The Card Shop

THE CARD SHOP

A Dazzling Collection of Handmade Paper Greetings

SANDRA LOUNSBURY FOOSE

author of *Simply Super Paper*

CB

CONTEMPORARY BOOKS

Library of Congress Cataloging-in-Publication Data

Foose, Sandra Lounsbury.
The card shop : a dazzling collection of handmade paper greetings / Sandra Lounsbury Foose.
p. cm.
ISBN 0-8092-2541-7
1. Greeting cards. I. Title.
TT872 .F66 2000
745.594'1—dc21 00-35830
CIP

Warning: When using cutting tools and other suggested products, readers are strongly cautioned to follow manufacturers' directions, to heed warnings, and to seek prompt medical attention for any injury. In addition, readers are warned to keep all potentially harmful supplies away from children.

Cover design by Monica Baziuk
Cover and interior photography by Sharon Hoogstraten
Interior design by Mary Lockwood
Interior illustrations by Sandra Lounsbury Foose

Published by Contemporary Books
A division of NTC/Contemporary Publishing Group, Inc.
4255 West Touhy Avenue, Lincolnwood (Chicago), Illinois 60712-1975 U.S.A.

Printed in Hong Kong by Midas Printing Ltd.
International Standard Book Number: 0-8092-2541-7
30 29 28 27 26 25 24 23 22 21 20 19 18 17 16 15 14 13 12 11 10 9 8 7 6 5 4 3 2 1

To Joyce,

For there is no friend like a sister
In calm or stormy weather;
To cheer one on the tedious way,
To fetch one if one goes astray,
To lift one if one totters down,
To strengthen whilst one stands.

CHRISTINA ROSSETTI 1862

Contents

Preface

Millions of little envelopes crisscross the country every day, each one carrying a message of love, joy, comfort, hope, encouragement, appreciation, apology, or concern. Sent out in every direction, the greeting cards tucked inside these envelopes arrive like tiny envoys and become paper keepsakes expressing our affection for one another.

Today most greeting cards are commercially produced; but increasingly many are handmade, just as they were long ago when all such tokens of affection were created by loving hands at home. An extra-special store-bought card is sometimes sent in place of a gift, but a handmade card is more than just a substitute for a present. It is a true gift in itself, for the one who receives it, as well as the one who creates it. The words of Eudora Welty so eloquently describe the pleasure of creating and receiving something made by hand: "We see human thought and feeling best and clearest by seeing it through something solid that our hands have made."

Creating handmade cards is a delightful and tangible way to share your thoughts and feelings with family, friends, and colleagues. For inspiration and instruction, *The Card Shop* focuses on creativity, simplicity, affordability, and fun! Starting with a visit to Studio Know-How (Chapter 1), you can learn or review essential information about paper, supplies, tools, and techniques. Then for year-round inspiration, browse through the pages of each seasonal chapter: Spring Greetings, Summer Wishes, Autumn Notes, and Winter Cheer, borrowing ideas from one season or another to suit your fancy and fulfill your needs. Several cards in the collection live double lives as ornaments, bookmarks, gift tags, or framable art. Some of the designs are three-dimensional, but each one can be folded flat to fit inside one of the five envelopes whose patterns are provided. With this book close at hand, you will always have your favorite card shop nearby—right at your fingertips. Best wishes!

—Sandra Lounsbury Foose

THE CARD SHOP

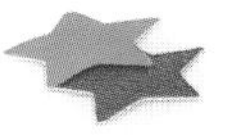

I

Studio Know-How

Studio Know-How

All you need to know can be found here in the studio section—paper, tools, terms, techniques, and even a list of suppliers. Some of this information will be new to you; but some of it will be a review. Those long-ago days you spent making snowflakes and valentines have already provided many of the skills and memories you will use to create your own wonderful cards today.

A Paper Primer

Art Paper: These high-quality, heavy-weight papers are made by Canson, Crescent, Canford, Strathmore, Fabriano, and other manufacturers. Richly hued, subtly textured art papers inspire the heart, eye, and hand. Unlike construction paper, which fades easily and splits when scored and folded, art paper holds its color and has good strength and memory. When art paper is scored and folded it will not crack or tear, and when it is curled and rolled it will keep its form.

Bond Paper: Available in white and a rainbow of wonderful colors, this is ordinary, inexpensive, stationery-weight paper, usually measuring 8½″ × 11″ (21.6 cm × 28.0 cm) in size. Fabulous colors with matching envelopes are often sold in copy shops.

Corrugated Paper: Since it is often used for protective packaging, sometimes you can rescue this textured paper from a recycling bin. When the corrugated texture is accidentally crushed, repair it by running a thin dowel or a bamboo skewer inside the tunnels and lifting up the dents. Corrugated paper is also known as corduroy paper.

Duplex Paper: This is a light- to medium-weight multipurpose paper with a different color on each side of a single sheet. Also known as duet paper, the duplex paper used in this book was made by Bemiss-Jason.

Foil Paper and Foil Board: Smooth and shiny or embossed with texture, metallic foil paper looks wonderful lining envelopes, and that's a great place to salvage it too! Working with brightly colored, high-gloss foil can be a bit rough on the eyes, especially at night, because of the glare created by artificial lighting. When you work with foil board, remember that once you score and fold it, the board beneath the foil surface will appear as a white line on your work.

Garden Paper: This soft, delightful, handmade paper is embedded with real flowers, leaves, and seeds, so no two pieces are ever alike.

Glassine Paper: This shiny, transparent material, somewhat similar to kitchen wax paper, is used to make envelopes for displaying and protecting paper collectables such as stamps. Available in about a dozen different sizes, the envelopes can be purchased in bulk and sometimes individually at stamp hobby shops.

Glow-in-the-Dark Paper: Luminescent paper is kind of a splurge because of its price, but it sure is fun to use! It cuts and folds like origami paper and every time it is exposed to light, it will glow brightly for at least thirty minutes afterward.

Graph Paper: Select graph paper with boldly printed inch lines and a grid size of either four squares per inch (4 × 4) or eight squares per inch (8 × 8). If you need a large piece for pattern making, tape smaller pieces together after overlapping and aligning the squares.

Japanese Papers: Only origami and chiyogami papers were used in this book. Traditional lightweight origami paper is easy to find in packages of brightly colored squares but it is also available in metallic foil, double-sided, iridescent, luminescent, opalescent, and Japanese folk-art print assortments. Chiyogami paper is strong, medium weight, and fade-resistant. It is silkscreened with exquisite repeating patterns. Chiyogami papers are brilliantly colored and soft and warm to the touch, very much like fabric.

Kraft Paper: Humble but handsome and easy to salvage, kraft paper is most often used for bagging groceries and wrapping parcels, because of its strength and low cost. Now and then you may encounter kraft paper enhanced with a printed design or brushed with a metallic wash, and the look is surprisingly elegant.

Lace Paper Doilies: Frosty white circles, squares, rectangles, ovals, and hearts of paper lace can be found in card shops, supermarkets, and places that sell party supplies.

Vellum: A medium-weight, high-quality, transparent paper, vellum is stronger than ordinary tracing paper. It makes interesting transparent envelopes that can actually be sent through the mail.

Velour Paper: Also known as flocked paper, velour paper has a soft, fuzzy, suedelike finish.

Wallpaper: Uncoated sheets of upscale wallpaper pulled from an old sample book were used to make several of the projects in this book. Wallpaper samples also make wonderful note cards, place mats, book covers, photo mats, and gift wraps.

Collecting Scraps

Without spending a single penny you can create a fabulous paper palette from scraps, leftovers, and throwaways.

Gift-giving occasions yield wrappings and boxes, ribbons and strings, as well as the colorful paper of greeting cards, envelopes, and their linings. Packaging materials worth salvaging could be lurking just inside the shopping bags and other merchandise you regularly carry home. Even the mailbox holds potential treasures in the forms of of advertisements, invitations, annual reports, garden catalogs, promotional mailings, and such. Check for unusual colors, patterns, and textures on folders, bags, stationery, calendars, playing cards, newspapers, maps, the covers of old notebooks, damaged sheets of music, and even lightbulb cartons with their corrugated inserts.

Search your community for other freebie possibilities. Many of the patterned papers you will see in this book were found in a discontinued wallpaper sample book about to be discarded by an interior-design shop in my small town. Local printers might have outdated or duplicate paper sample books that could be yours for the asking. Usually these swatch books are also available at paper superstores and paper wholesalers. After carefully removing the samples from the books (watch those staples), you will often find that the swatches are large enough to make complete projects. In fact, nearly half the projects in this book were made with just such salvaged scraps.

The Work Box

Collect all of these pieces of basic equipment and stash them together in a big box, a sturdy basket, a tote bag, or a plastic storage container. For safety's sake, if there are little children in your home, be sure to keep your work box out of their reach. Every time you make a project you will need to use at least one item from your work box. Since you will have all these things stored together and close at hand, most of the items in the work box won't appear again on the materials list provided for each project.

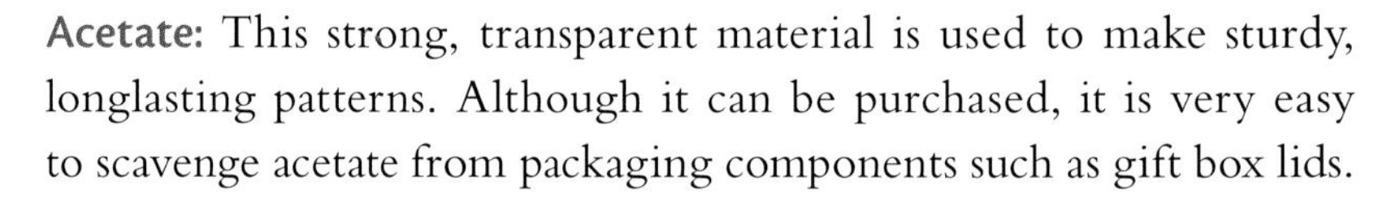

Acetate: This strong, transparent material is used to make sturdy, longlasting patterns. Although it can be purchased, it is very easy to scavenge acetate from packaging components such as gift box lids.

Clip Clothespins: Clothespins are perfect for holding glued pieces of paper together while they dry. They also function as giant paper clips, keeping your patterns, papers, and notes organized.

Compass: An ordinary pencil-holding compass is adequate for drawing circles, but a multi-use clip compass is even better because it will hold a marker or a craft knife. For the greatest cutting accuracy, however, I prefer an adjustable-arm circle cutter.

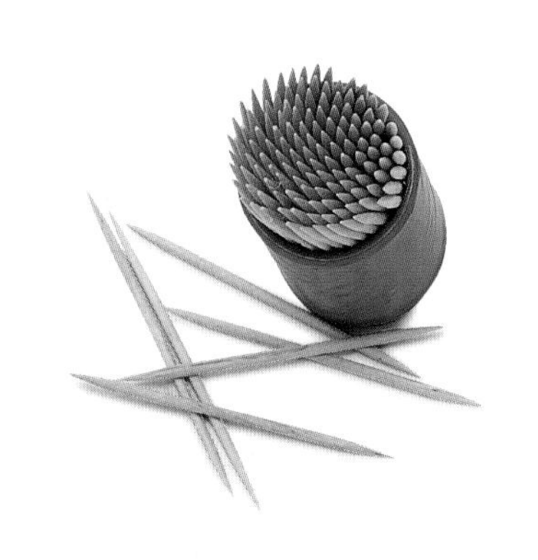

Cotton Swabs: When dampened just a little bit, a cotton swab is the perfect tool for removing glue spots.

Craft Knife with Replacement Blades: Scissors can be used for some of the projects, but many involve delicate, precision cutting and require the use of a craft knife with a #11 blade. Select a knife with a soft, rubberized (preferably contoured) barrel for comfort and control, an antiroll device, and a cap for safety. The knife should also have a safe and easy blade release mechanism. In order to protect your most precious tools—your own two hands—avoid all other cutting devices. Children should not use craft knives.

Crochet Cotton, Pearl Cotton, Thread, Ribbon, and String: Available in craft and fabric shops, these fiber materials are most often used to make hanging loops on ornaments or details on other projects.

Cutting Mat: Heavy cardboard can be used for a temporary cutting mat, but it will wear out very quickly and dull the blade of your craft knife. Self-healing rotary cutting mats are really made for rotary cutters, and they forget how to heal when a craft blade mars the surface. The very best resilient cutting base has a translucent, semihard, rubberlike surface that accepts the blade and then miraculously heals itself. The cutting mat, manufactured by Alvin, is nonslip, nonglare, and conveniently marked with a 1″ grid pattern. It heals so completely that I use it as both a drawing surface and a cutting surface. This is a pricey item, but worth the investment.

Eraser: With gentle pressure, a nonabrasive white vinyl eraser removes pencil lines cleanly, without smudging. For precise work the most convenient form is an eraser that resembles a mechanical pencil and can also be refilled.

Felt-Tip Pens: An inexpensive, basic set of fine-line felt-tip markers is adequate. Test markers on paper to check for feathering of color.

Glue: Every project in this collection was made with an Elmer's All-Purpose Glue Stick (not the Craft Glue Stick or the School Glue Stick). This adhesive dries clear and makes a strong bond. It also dries quickly but not instantly, so if you work fast you can make small adjustments. Always try a test patch of glue on your good paper.

Monofilament: This soft, invisible, nylon sewing thread is used to make some of the ornament projects.

Needles and Pins: Needles and pins are most often used to pierce holes in patterns so construction details can be inconspicuously transferred onto your paper with tiny pencil dots. Occasionally pins and needles are used to make pierced design details directly on a project, so you should have a variety of sizes, some quite thin and some chunky. "T" pins are a good choice, because the "T" bar at the top serves as a little handle, making the pin easy to hold.

Paper Clips: These can be real time-savers when used to hold glued layers of paper together to dry. To avoid scratching your work, use paper clips with care and remove them promptly so they don't leave any rust marks.

Paper Punches: Metal plier-type paper punches are available in ⅛″ (0.3 cm), 3⁄16″ (0.5 cm), and ¼″ (0.6 cm) diameters. All three sizes are

Optional Equipment

Drawing Board: To make the projects in this book, a drawing board with T-square and triangles is not essential, but such supplies do ensure accuracy and efficiency. If you consider such a purchase, a white plastic Koh-I-Noor® Studio Drawing Board with a paper clamp and a removable transparent sliding straightedge acting as a T-square on it is affordable and more than adequate. To complete the set, use separately purchased inexpensive 6″ (15.2 cm) 30°/60° and 45°/90° plastic triangles on the board. Neither the plastic board nor the plastic triangles should be used with a craft knife.

Erasable Transfer Paper: Used like carbon paper to transfer patterns, this is a waxless, greaseless, smudge-proof material. Graphite and white transfer paper are made in reusable 18″ × 36″ (45.8 cm × 91.5 cm) sheets. It's best to have one of each color.

The Essential Work Box

Clip clothespins

Compass

Cotton swabs

Craft knife and package of #11 replacement blades

Cutting mat, self-healing type or sheets of thick cardboard (not corrugated)

Eraser, nonabrasive white vinyl

Elmer's All-Purpose Glue Stick

Needles and pins

Paper clips

Pencil sharpener, very good quality, handheld type

Pencils with erasers for drawing; white pencil

Rulers 6″ (15.2 cm) and 12″ (30.5 cm), or 18″ (45.8 cm)

Scissors, 7″ (17.8 cm) student or all-purpose; 5″ (12.7 cm) embroidery scissors

Straightedge, metal, 18″ (45.8 cm) or 24″ (61.0 cm)

Tape, both transparent and removable

Toothpicks

Tracing paper

Tweezers

used for projects in this book, but if you have trouble finding the 3⁄16″ (0.5 cm) diameter, the 1⁄4″ (0.6 cm) size could be substituted. Decorative paper punches are great for quickly producing a variety of cut confetti shapes, such as hearts, stars, and butterflies.

Pencil Sharpener: A quality handheld sharpener with a twist-off barrel to empty shavings will help keep your desk and your work neat.

Pencils: You will need a traditional #2 wooden school pencil with a soft graphite lead for tracing patterns and transferring patterns onto paper. A white coloring pencil is essential for transferring patterns onto dark paper.

Ruler: I like to work with flat metal rulers and use a 6″ (15.2 cm) and a 12″ (30.5 cm) for most projects. Consider purchasing a safety ruler, which can serve double duty as a measuring device as well as a straightedge when cutting with a craft knife. Safety rulers have nonskid backings and are especially designed so there is a barrier between your fingers and the knife.

Scissors: When selecting scissors, it is very important to consider comfort as well as size. Try them before you buy them. For general use I favor lightweight, all purpose, 7″ (17.8 cm) Fiskars® scissors, with molded plastic handles suitable for right-handed or left-handed use. For delicate and precise work I use 5″ (12.7 cm) pointed-tip embroidery scissors. Paper edgers are used for cutting decorative borders. Dozens of designs are available, but only the scallop and the zigzag edgers were used in this book.

Straightedge: A metal straightedge is required to safely cut paper with a craft knife. It must protect your fingers, so look for one with a nonskid backing and a barrier or a lip on one of its edges.

Tape: Transparent tape is occasionally used to hold paper pieces together and to reinforce delicate scoring lines. Removable tape is used when making patterns.

Toothpicks: When adding bits of glue in tight places, toothpicks are helpful tools.

Tracing Paper: When you do not photocopy patterns, use this lightweight, transparent paper to trace the patterns directly from the book. Purchase an 8½″ × 11″ (21.6 cm × 27.9 cm) or a 9″ × 12″ (22.8 cm × 30.5 cm) pad. If you need a larger piece of paper, tape the small sheets together.

Tweezers: Use tweezers to move tiny pieces of paper into position and to hold hard-to-reach layers of paper together while drying.

Tricks & Techniques

"If all else fails, read the directions." I don't know who first offered that advice, but I know many who take it to heart! Granted, the best lessons do sometimes come from our worst mistakes. Generally speaking, however, taking the time to review basic information at the beginning of an activity is a better way to learn, so please read on.

Making Patterns: Some projects are best made with photocopied patterns, but most can be traced directly from the book. Hold the tracing paper in place on the page with paper clips or small pieces of removable tape. Strive for accuracy when tracing, because a well-made pattern will ensure the best results. Check your straight-sided patterns for precision by holding them against graph paper. On the patterns, continuous solid lines are always cutting lines, dotted lines show placement of a detail or another piece, and broken lines indicate folding lines. Label all patterns and keep them clipped together or tucked into separate envelopes.

To strengthen patterns or make very tiny ones easier to handle, glue the pieces to acetate before cutting them out. When using a craft knife, it is not always necessary to cut straight through the acetate. Sometimes you can just score it on the pattern line and then complete the job by breaking the acetate on the scored line.

Transferring Details: Pattern shapes and details can be transferred onto the project paper in several ways.

The first method involves using a needle or a pin to pierce the pattern details, such as faces and folding lines, before the pattern is placed on the project paper. The details can then be transferred directly onto the paper by placing a very sharp pencil inside the pattern holes.

Using commercial transfer paper is another efficient method. Transfer paper is usually very responsive to pressure, so draw gently over the pattern lines, but always test the product on a scrap of your good paper before you use it.

Maintaining Supplies

Treat your paper collection with care. Store the sheets flat. You can make a hinged storage portfolio for large papers by using tape to join two same-size pieces of cardboard together along one edge. Sort smaller pieces of paper by color in folders, bags, or envelopes, but before you squirrel them away, remove all traces of tape so the adhesive residue will not mar the texture or discolor the paper surface.

Rolling paper for storage is not a good idea, but if you absolutely must do it, roll the pieces very loosely and don't put rubber bands, tape, or paper clips on them. Instead, wrap a strip of scrap paper around the roll and use a piece of tape to attach the strip to itself. If paper is difficult to flatten after being rolled, gently re-roll it in the opposite direction.

Keep paper out of the sun and away from moisture and be sure your hands are very clean and dry before you touch it. Dust, fingerprints, and graphite smudges are difficult to remove; color fading is irreversible.

Although it is easier said than done, keep your work area neat and clean. Only set up the items you need for the project at hand and keep your supplies clean too. Replace the cap on the glue. Store your tapes in plastic bags to keep the edges clean. Wash your hands after using pencils and glue. Don't use your drawing board for a snack tray.

If you are unable to find erasable transfer paper, here's one more transfer method. After tracing the pattern from the book, cut out the pattern, flip it over, and redraw the details on the reverse side of the pattern, right on top of the original detail lines. Then flip the pattern over again so the right side of it faces you. Place the pattern on the paper of your choice. Draw around the pattern and transfer the details by drawing on top of the detail lines again.

Determining Paper Grain: Machine-made papers usually have a grain, which is a built-in directional preference based on the arrangement of the paper fibers. This structural quality makes it easier to fold or tear paper in one direction than in the other, say top to bottom, rather than side to side. Creasing a paper with the grain makes the cleanest folding line. Folds made across or against the grain sometimes appear uneven and ragged. Several projects require that folds be made in both directions and when that occurs, scoring the paper before folding will help to ensure a good appearance. The easiest way to test a paper's grain is to bring two of its parallel edges together, bending the paper at the middle without folding it. Then release the bend, rotate the paper a quarter turn, and bring the remaining two parallel edges together. The paper will show more resistance to being bent in one direction than the other. The grain runs parallel to the edges that are easiest to bring together, so a fold made parallel to those edges would be made with the grain.

Using Tape: Removable tape or paper clips are used to hold patterns on the project paper. Keep in mind that most tape is extremely rough on wallpaper. It's always wise to start by making a test patch of tape on your good paper to see if it mars the surface or leaves a sticky residue.

Erasing Drawings: Rough erasing will mar or tear the surface of some papers and remove the color or make shiny spots on others. Use a light touch when drawing patterns so you won't need to remove heavy lines. If you must use an eraser, make slow strokes in one direction, instead of scrubbing the area at top speed.

Cutting Paper: Practice cutting paper scraps with a craft knife, and find the way to hold it that gives you the greatest control and comfort. Never let yourself become careless with knives and blades.

To cut or score straight lines with a craft knife, always use a nonslip safety ruler or a straightedge as a barrier between your fingers and the blade. When cutting or scoring curved lines, keep moving the paper, instead of the knife, and place your fingers away from the path of the blade. If working on a small piece of paper brings your hand too close to the knife, securely tape the small piece of paper onto a bigger piece of cardboard. Always keep your eyes and your full attention on the blade.

When you are cutting multiple duplicate shapes together, stack the papers and use tape or clips to hold each layer of paper securely to the next. If the layers are not bound together, they will shift as pressure is applied to the knife, and distorted shapes will result. When cutting through multiple layers of paper, it is safer to make several successive cuts with gentle pressure rather than trying to cut through all the layers with one heavy-handed pass of the knife. It is hazardous to use a dull blade or one with even a tiny piece of the tip broken off. These conditions diminish your control of the knife and they will ruin the paper, tearing it instead of cutting it. Carefully wrap a used blade in masking tape before disposing of it responsibly.

For the greatest accuracy when cutting curves with scissors, keep the scissors stationary, without moving the wrist as you move the paper into the cutting blades, instead of keeping the paper stationary and moving the scissors around it.

Scoring Folding Lines: It is easy to make a crisp fold on lightweight origami paper, but medium-weight and heavy paper must be first scored in order to fold neatly. To score, move the craft knife along an accurately drawn folding line (broken line on pattern) making a very shallow groove in the paper without cutting through it. Within the groove, the knife breaks only the very top fibers of the paper, enabling it to fold with ease and precision. Use a metal safety straightedge whenever you score folding lines. When scoring curved lines, move the paper instead of the knife as you follow the line. Small pieces are easiest to score before they are cut out.

Some projects require scoring on the front of the piece; others need scoring on the reverse side. The instructions will tell you when and where to score. Paper is usually bent away from a scored line. When you see the term "mountain fold," the folding line is marked and scored on the right side of the paper and then the paper is bent away from you to create the peak of an imaginary mountain. When you see the term "valley fold," the folding line is marked and scored on the reverse side of the paper and then the paper is flipped over to the right side and bent toward you to make a little valley. To create an accordion-folded piece of paper, make alternating parallel mountain and valley folds on it. To protect your paper, use a cover sheet of tracing paper over your work when creasing or flattening it. Be

Mail-Order Catalogs

If you request all of these catalogs, you will be able to find just about everything used in this book. There might be a charge for some of the catalogs, but sometimes it is refunded with the first order. Ask about the return policy of each company.

Dick Blick Art Material
Department SF
P.O. Box 1267
Galesburg, IL 61402-1267
1-800-828-4548

Home-Sew Sewing and Craft Supplies
P.O. Box 4099
Bethlehem, PA 18018-0099
1-800-344-4739 Fax: 610-867-9717

The Japanese Paper Place
887 Queen Street West
Toronto, Ontario
Canada M6J 1G5
413-703-0089 Fax: 413-703-0163
www.interlog.com/~washi/>

Kate's Paperie
561 Broadway
New York, NY 10012
1-888-941-9169

NASCO Arts and Crafts
East of the Rockies:
901 Janesville Avenue
Fort Atkinson, WI 53538-0901
1-800-558-9595
West of the Rockies:
4825 Stoddard Road
Modesto, CA 95356-9318
1-800-558-9595

Sax Arts and Crafts
P.O. Box 510710
New Berlin, WI 53151
1-800-558-6696
www.saxarts.com

Keeping in Touch

As the saying goes, "a picture is worth a thousand words"—which is why your handmade card will say a lot for you even if you only sign your name! But since a greeting card often takes the place of a letter, visit, or telephone call, the message enclosed within it is of great significance.

At right are some simple suggestions for messages for your cards. Trust your own voice, and let your heart help you put your thoughts on paper.

If you need more ideas, remember that your library is full of books of quotations, poetry, and even jokes. I especially love to use quotes from Shakespeare, Emily Dickinson, the Bible, and my favorite hymns. Inspiration also abounds in the titles and lyrics of music. Look around and collect verses in the same way you would collect paper, and always credit the source.

Happy Heart Day!

Hug enclosed

You are my sunshine.

Love is in the air.

My heart is filled with love for you.

I love the thought of you.

Wherever you go, my love is there.

You warm my heart.

You mean so much to me.

My heart belongs to you.

You make my heart sing!

Dear to my heart you'll always be.

You are precious to me.

S.W.A.K.

Two hearts, one love

Together is a wonderful place to be.

Happy trails to you!

May you live "happily ever after."

Best wishes for a wonderful life together.

May all your dreams come true.

Hoppy Easter!

Everybunny loves you!

Hugs and kisses and springtime wishes

Welcome little one.

Dreams really do come true.

The best things come in small packages!

Little things mean a lot!

Happy Pappy's Day

Home is where the Mom is.

How did God know I wanted you for my mommy?

especially careful when scoring and folding wallpaper, because it may crack. If this happens, mend or reinforce a weak area by placing a piece of transparent tape on the reverse side of the trouble spot.

Adding Glue: Sometimes glue can change the color of the paper or bubble its surface, so always make a glue test patch on the paper of your choice, and allow it to dry thoroughly before you proceed. Spread a thin layer of glue quickly and uniformly, using a pin, toothpick, popsicle stick, or folded index card as a tool, depending on the size of the work. After joining glued surfaces, place a clean sheet of tracing paper (a cover sheet) over the work to protect it, and then rub the area to smooth it and distribute the glue. Do the smoothing with your fingertips, or roll a glue-stick tube on it, or pull your

When I count my blessings, I think of you.

Thanks for the memories!

You shouldn't have, but I'm glad you did!

Your kindness warms my heart.

Thanks for all you do.

You're an angel.

Remembering our special times together

I'm so glad there's you!

Friend to me you'll always be.

I'm here when you need me.

Friends like you are precious and few.

You are in my thoughts and prayers.

Thinking of you with love.

Count your blessings not your years.

It's your day to shine!

Let's party!

Bon Voyage!

Adios, amigos!

What's cooking?

Well done!

Magnifico!

You did it!

Follow your dreams!

The sky is the limit!

Happy Trick-or-Treating!

Best Witches!

Love to my little pumpkin

Boo!

Happy BooDay to you.

You are so bootiful!

Take time to be thankful.

Enjoy life's simple blessings.

Count your blessings.

Celebrate the Season!

Peace Hope Love Joy

Have yourself a merry little Christmas!

Warm Winter Wishes

Peace on Earth, Goodwill to All

Joy to the World!

Shalom

May love and light fill your heart and home.

May this beautiful season bring joy to your home and a song to your heart.

straightedge over the joint. Then remove the cover sheet and use paper clips or clothespins to hold the layers of the glued area together until dry. Alternatively, sandwich the piece between two layers of tracing paper and place it under a stack of heavy books until it is dry. Elmer's All-Purpose Glue Stick will dry clear, but it might leave shiny spots on your work. If so, use a damp, not wet, cotton swab to carefully wipe away the dried glue. Keep the opposite cotton end dry so it can be used to smooth the dampened area and absorb excess moisture. First try the dampened swab on a scrap piece and you will see if moisture mars the paper surface or causes the color to bleed. Sometimes it's just better to leave the glue spot. Transparent tape should not be used in place of glue, because it discolors, becomes brittle, and loses its adhesive quality with age.

2

Spring Greetings

Kite Card

On the string tail of this little kite a flock of simple, folded origami birds perches in place of the traditional rag ties. The kite's crosswise bridle string doubles as a hanging loop so the card can be enjoyed as a miniature mobile when hung near a window to catch the breeze.

Instructions

1. Trace pattern and cut out.
2. Hold pattern in place on paper with tape or clips. Draw around shape and remove pattern. Use craft knife on protected surface to cut out kite. Repeat to make two kite shapes.

Materials

For one 4″ × 4⅝″ (10.2 cm × 11.7 cm) card

Pattern on page 85

Equipment in work box, pages 4–6

Two 4¼″ × 5″ (10.8 cm × 12.7 cm) pieces of sturdy paper for kite

12½″ (31.8 cm) length of lightweight string

Three 2″ (5.1 cm) squares of lightweight origami paper for birds

Black fine-line felt-tip pen

Envelope, 4⅜″ × 5¾″ (11.1 cm × 14.6 cm), or Envelope B pattern, page 82, and instructions, pages 80–82

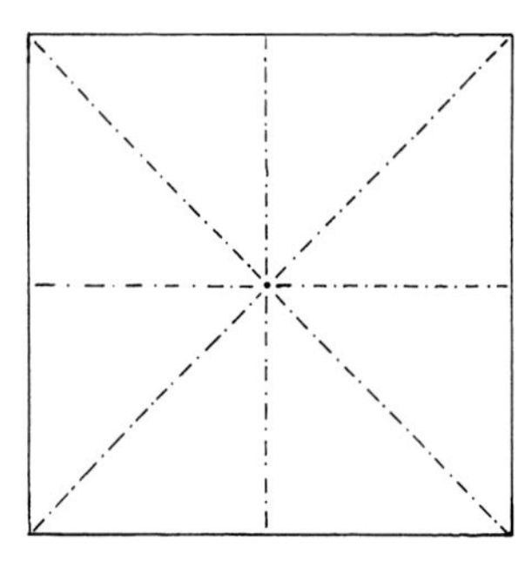

1. To make bird, fold paper in half horizontally and unfold. Fold paper in half vertically and unfold. Fold paper in half diagonally in one direction and unfold. Fold paper in half diagonally in the other direction and unfold. Fold lines should resemble drawing.

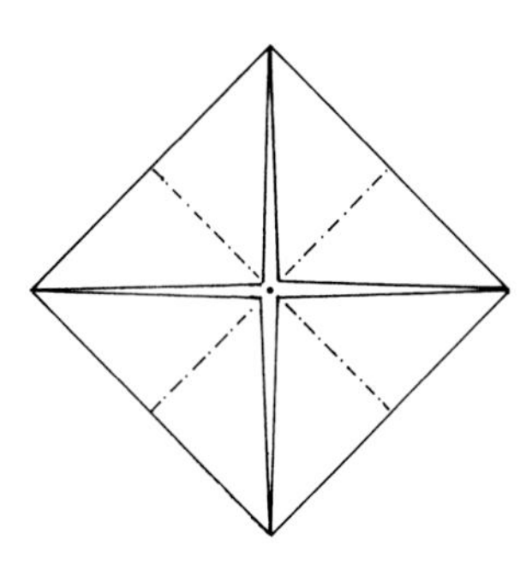

2. Place paper white side up on work surface. Draw a tiny dot at center of paper. Fold up each corner to meet this dot and crease folds.

3. On reverse side of one kite piece score and fold crosswise folding line. Cut 7″ (17.8 cm) length of string, reserving remaining piece. Referring to kite drawing at right, glue 7″ (17.8 cm) piece of string within glue area of this same kite piece. Allow to dry. Reserve remaining unfolded kite piece.
4. Spread glue on entire glue area above crosswise folding line, covering string ends with glue as well. Place reserved unfolded kite piece on top of glue area, aligning all edges. Allow to dry.
5. Refer to Drawings 1 through 10 to make origami birds. Use felt-tip pen to draw eyes on birds.
6. To make kite tail, glue one end of reserved portion of string inside card. Space birds evenly on string, and attach them to string by using pin to spread thin line of glue precisely down center back of each bird. Hold in place until dry.

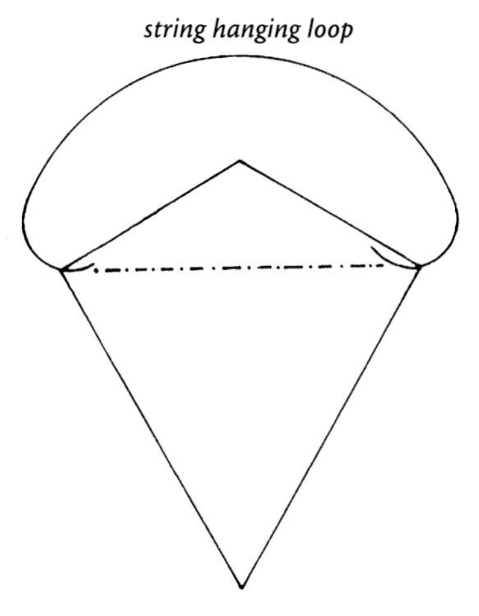

Score and crease folding line on inside of card back. Glue string hanging loop in place.

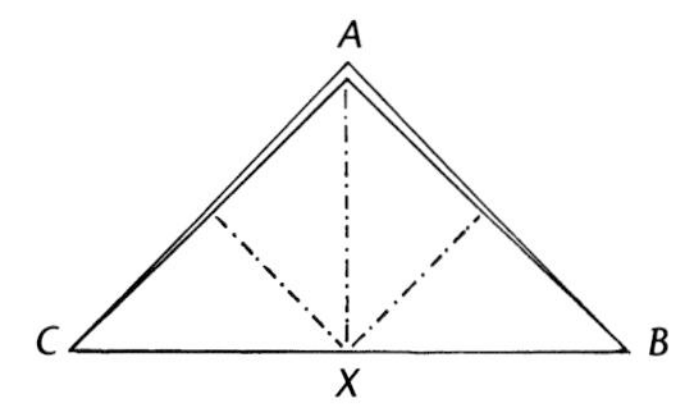

3. Make triangular unit by folding lowest corner of folded square up to meet highest corner. Label corners of triangle A, B, and C as indicated on drawing. Label center bottom X.

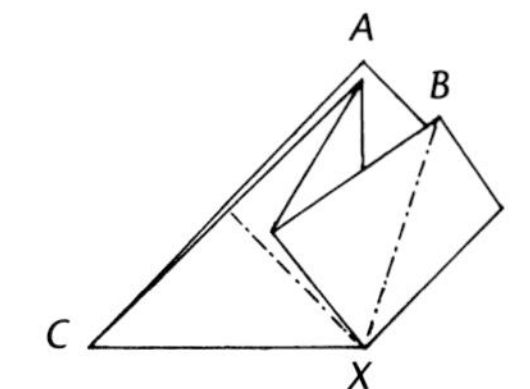

4. Lift and push point B up to point A, folding unit on preexisting folding lines.

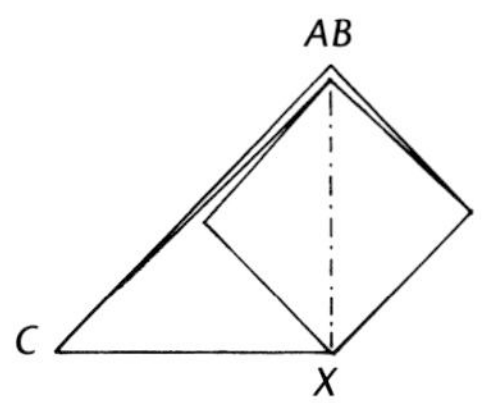

5. Crease folding lines sharply.

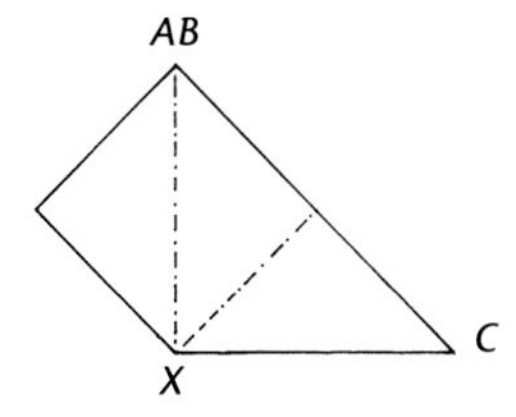

6. Flip unit to reverse side.

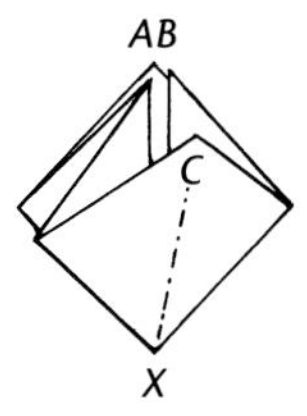

7. Lift and push point C up to point AB, folding unit on preexisting folding lines. Crease folding lines sharply.

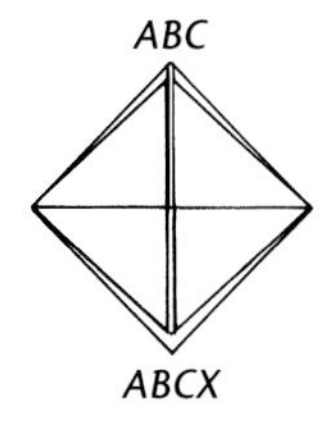

8. To form one wing, fold down one layer of point ABC to meet point X.

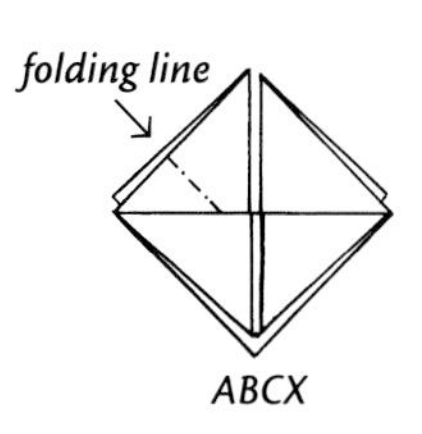

9. To make other wing, flip unit to reverse side and again fold down one layer of point ABC to meet point X.

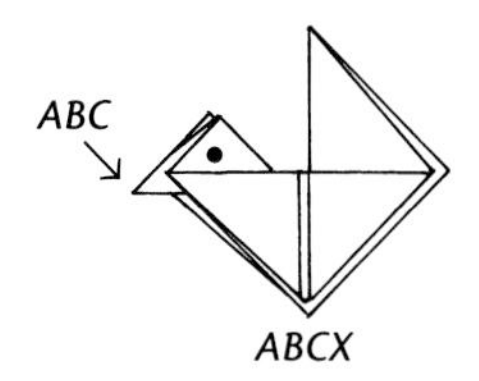

10. Noting broken folding line sketched on Drawing 9, push down on one of points remaining at top of unit and pull it slightly forward outside of bird to create beak. Crease sharply on sketched folding line to form head.

Tick-Tack-Toe Valentine

Materials

For one 4¼″ (10.8 cm) square card

Pattern on page 85

Equipment in work box, pages 4–6

4¼″ × 8½″ (10.8 cm × 21.6 cm) piece of sturdy duplex paper

Envelope, 4⅜″ × 5¾″ (11.1 cm × 14.6 cm), or Envelope B pattern, page 82, and instructions, pages 80–82

Fill all the spaces of this tick-tack-toe card with hugs and kisses for your valentine. This is an easy card to make and it is fun to watch the lacy pattern appear as you cut away the negative spaces around the letters.

Instructions

1. Trace or photocopy pattern and trim around square.
2. Score and fold paper in half crosswise. Unfold. Tape paper crosswise onto work surface with outside of card facing up. Tape pattern in place to right of folding line, aligning edges of pattern with card front.
3. Using craft knife and straightedge, cut out and discard negative areas on card.

Folded Heart Card

Express your love on Valentine's Day or convey your best wishes for a marriage or anniversary with this folded heart card. To add an extra-special touch, place a small photograph on the back panel and the heart will serve as a miniature picture frame.

Instructions

1. Tape each paper square onto protected work surface. The desired color of folded triangular tabs around edges should face up because cutting and scoring of folding lines will be done on reverse side of each heart.
2. Rough cut each heart pattern and tape one to each paper square. Cutting directly through pattern and duplex paper, cut on all solid lines including heart outlines. Discard negative center portions of heart 1 and heart 2. Referring to pattern, score all folding lines (broken lines on pattern).
3. Turn hearts over to reverse (card front) side. Fold each triangular tab to front. Place tracing paper over each completely folded heart to protect it, and pull straightedge across work to sharply crease all folding lines.
4. Apply no glue to top heart 1. On middle heart 2, apply glue to top X-marked tabs. Align top heart 1 on middle heart 2 and press together so X-marked tabs become hinges for two heart layers. Apply glue to top X-marked tabs on bottom heart 3. Align glued card unit on bottom heart 3 and press together. Allow to dry. Tabs at base of each heart can be unfolded if necessary to stabilize card when it stands. Take special care when inserting card in envelope.

Materials

For one 3¼″ × 3½″ (8.2 cm × 8.9 cm) card

Photocopy of patterns on page 86

Equipment in work box, pages 4–6

One 4″ (10.2 cm) square of duplex paper for each of three hearts

Envelope, 4¼″ × 5⅛″ (10.8 cm × 13.0 cm), or Envelope C pattern, page 83, and instructions, pages 80–83

Dove Note

Let this simple folk-art dove carry your love notes, announcements, or invitations all through the sweetheart season. Use a bright pastel paper for the heart and printed parchment paper for the lacy translucent envelope, or line a plain envelope with beautifully patterned paper for a different look.

Materials

For one 3½″ × 4¹³⁄₁₆″ (8.9 cm × 12.2 cm) card

Patterns on page 87

Equipment in work box, pages 4-6

5″ × 7½″ (12.7 cm × 19.1 cm) piece of sturdy paper

1½″ × 2½″ (3.8 cm × 6.4 cm) piece of lightweight paper

Paper punch, ⅛″ (0.3 cm) diameter

Envelope, 4¼″ × 5⅛″ (10.8 cm × 13.0 cm), or Envelope C pattern, page 83, and instructions, pages 80-83

Instructions

1. Trace or photocopy patterns and cut out. Punch out eye. Pierce detail lines in several places with pin.
2. Score and fold both papers in half crosswise. Use sturdy folded paper to make dove, aligning "place on fold" edge of pattern with folded edge of paper. Hold pattern in place with tape or paper clips. Draw around outside edge and transfer details by placing sharp pencil in pinholes. Remove pattern. Tape or clip paper layers together. Cut out dove using craft knife on protected work surface. Cut horizontal beak and feather lines. Punch out eye.
3. Use lightweight paper to make heart following method previously described for dove. Slide heart into dove beak on card front.

Egg Bunny Card

Lift the front of this Easter egg and discover a bunny surprise inside. Swing the card front to the back of the bunny and it becomes a prop, helping the bunny to stand.

Instructions

1. Photocopy or trace patterns and cut out. Cut out or punch out circles for eyes. Cut curved mouth line.
2. Using tape or paper clips hold egg and bunny patterns in place on printed side of paper. Draw around shapes, transferring folding lines. Remove patterns.
3. Using craft knife on protected work surface, cut out bunny and slice between ears and feet. Also cut out egg. On printed side of bunny, score and fold curved lines on ears. Also score folding lines along feet, arms, and base of ears. On printed side of egg, score two parallel folding lines at base of glue tab. On white side of bunny use pattern as template to transfer eyes and mouth line. Draw features with pen. When dry, fold bunny ears, arms, and feet against white egg-shaped body. Place glue on white side of egg glue tab. Center egg on folded bunny. Fold glue tab to printed side of bunny behind folded ears. Allow to dry.
4. From yellow paper cut two yolks and glue one to white side of bunny and one to white side of egg.

Materials

For one 2¼″ × 2¾″ (5.7 cm × 6.9 cm) card

Patterns on page 87

Equipment in work box, pages 4–6

4½″ × 9″ (11.4 cm × 22.8 cm) piece of sturdy patterned paper, white on reverse side

2″ × 4″ (5.1 cm × 10.2 cm) piece of yellow paper

Fine-line felt-tip marker

Paper punch, ⅛″ (0.3 cm) diameter

Envelope, 3⅞″ × 5⅜″ (9.8 cm × 13.6 cm), or Envelope E pattern, page 84, and instructions, pages 80–84

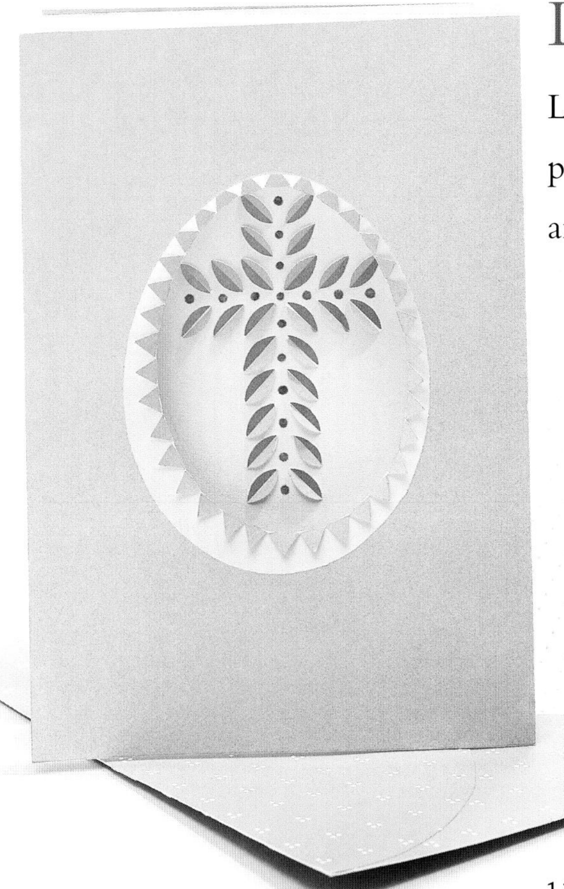

Leaf Cross Card

Leaves cut and folded on a piece of pastel duplex paper form the symbol of the cross within an egg on this card, perfect for Easter and other springtime celebrations.

Materials

For one 3¾″ × 5¼″ (9.5 cm × 13.3 cm) folded card

Photocopy of patterns on page 88

Equipment in work box, pages 4–6

8½″ × 11″ (21.6 cm × 27.9 cm) piece of lightweight duplex paper

Fine-line felt-tip pen

Envelope, 3⅞″ × 5⅜″ (9.8 cm × 13.6 cm), or Envelope E pattern, page 84, and instructions, pages 80–84

Instructions

1. Cut out pattern section A consisting of panel 1 and panel 2. To make pattern section B, first cut out panel 3. Then cut another piece of paper the same size as panel 3, omitting design. This is panel 4. Tape panel 3 and panel 4 together for pattern section B. Tape section A and section B together to make complete pattern for card. Accuracy is very important when making patterns for this project. Check for precise alignment of designs by referring to Drawing 1 and using the following directions to accordion-fold pattern into card format. Score and fold panel 1 on top of panel 2. Score and fold panel 2 over panel 3 and then panel 3 over panel 4. Hold folded card up to a lighted window to check alignment of design motifs on each panel. If edges of card and design motifs don't align, make adjustments.
2. Cut duplex paper in half crosswise. Place each piece on work surface horizontally, side by side. On right of work surface, paper color for card front should face up. On left of work surface, paper color for card front should face down. To join papers, draw line for glue tab ¼″ (0.6 cm) from left edge of paper on right of work surface. Score pencil line and spread glue along this edge. Overlap glued edge of this paper with edge of paper on left, aligning edge with scored line of glue tab. Two different color surfaces will be facing you, as in Drawing 2. This is inside surface of card.
3. Referring to Drawing 3, tape pattern on top of duplex paper, aligning folding line between panels 2 and 3 precisely with line formed at center of duplex paper where two colors are joined. Trace around outside edge of card. Mark vertical folding lines with a few tiny pinholes. Leave pattern in place. Using craft knife and making cuts through pattern, cut out oval on panel 1 and notched oval on panel 2. On panel 3, cut only

curved edge of each leaf. Remove pattern from card and reserve pattern to use again in next step. Cut out card. On panel 3, lightly score folding line on each leaf. Fold leaves back to reverse side of panel 3. Set card aside.

4. On panel 2 of reserved pattern, cut around scoring line at base of notches to make smooth oval template. Flip reserved, unfolded card to reverse side. This is outside surface of card. Using adjusted pattern with oval cutout, draw light pencil line to mark oval score line at base of notches on panel 2. Lightly score pencil line. Fold down notches to inside of card. Score vertical folding lines between panels 1 and 2 and between panels 3 and 4. Referring to pattern and photograph, use felt-tip pen to draw berries on panel 3. Fold card, referring again to Drawing 1.

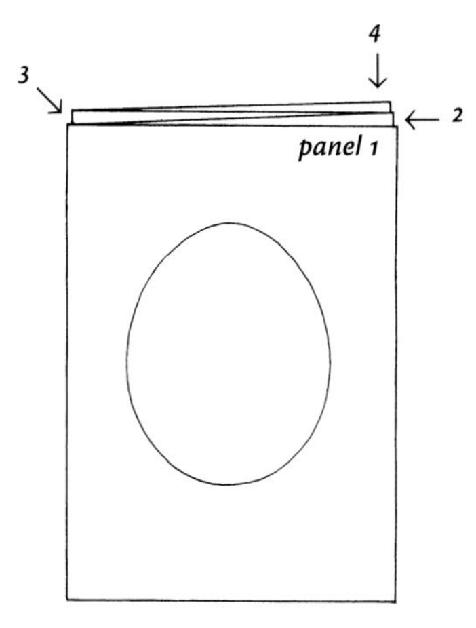

1. Accordion-fold pattern to align design motifs.

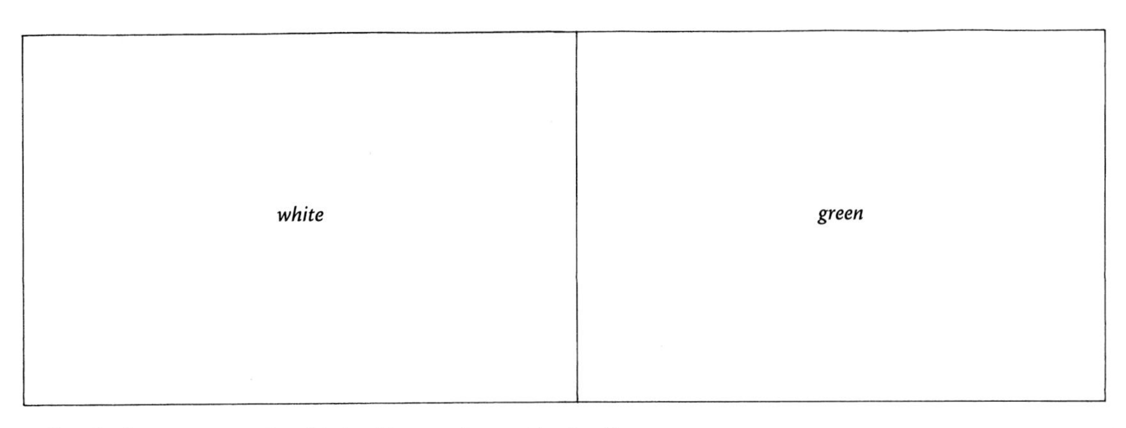

2. Glue duplex papers together side by side to make combined unit.

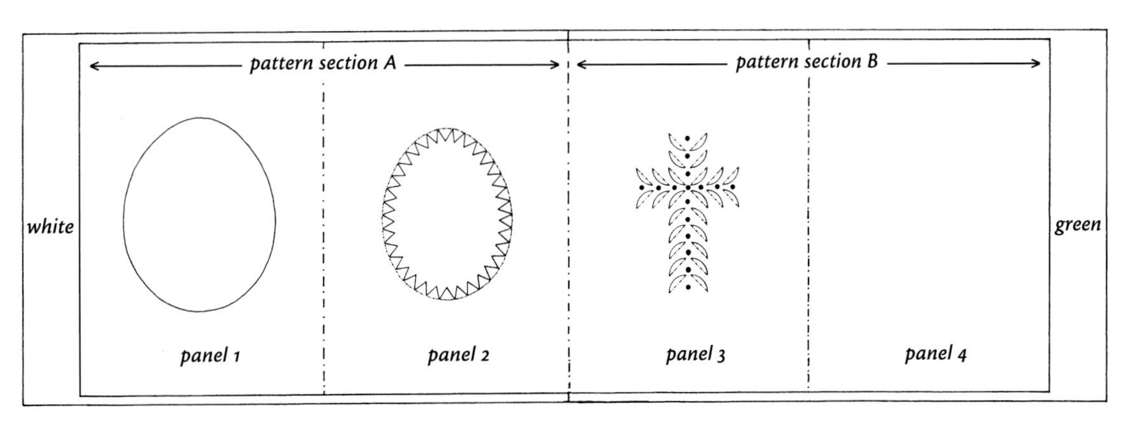

3. Tape pattern on duplex-paper unit.

Tea for Two Cards

Materials

For one 3½″ × 5½″ (8.9 cm × 14.0 cm) note

Large teapot pattern on page 89

Equipment in work box, pages 4–6

Two 4″ × 6″ (10.2 cm × 15.2 cm) pieces of sturdy paper for teapot

2″ (5.1 cm) square piece of paper for teabags, optional

Heart-shaped paper punch, 1″ (2.5 cm) diameter for teabags, optional

4″ (10.2 cm) length of string, optional

Envelope, 3⅝″ × 6½″ (9.2 cm × 16.5 cm), or Envelope D pattern, page 83, and instructions, pages 80–83

One of my favorite Saturday adventures is an early morning search for garage sale treasures. Old teapots are especially irresistible to me because of their pleasing designs as well as the comfort and friendship they symbolize. Use this teapot pattern in two different ways to send a cup of cheer to someone dear.

Teapot Note

Instructions

1. To make card front, refer to Drawing 1 and trace or photocopy complete large teapot pattern. Use needle or pin to pierce straight line of lid and curved side lines at spout and handle. Cut out pattern. To make card back, refer to Drawing 2, tracing same shape without spout and handle.

1. Trace full teapot shape for card front.

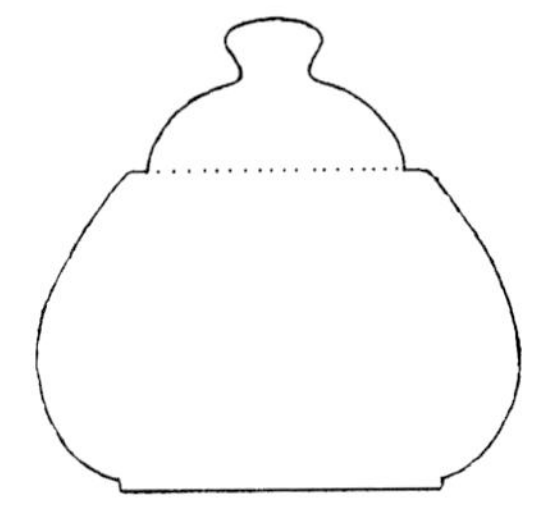

2. Trace teapot without spout and handle for card back.

2. Use tape or clips to hold patterns in place on large paper squares. Draw around each pattern lightly, transferring dots with sharp pencil tip. Cut out card front and back. Use pen or pencil to draw lines at lid, spout, and handle.
3. If you wish to add teabags use paper punch to cut out four heart shapes. Sandwich string ends between two glued hearts. Use large needle to pierce hole in full teapot shape (card front) along lid line. Pull string through hole, adjust length, and tape string to reverse side of card front.
4. On reverse side of card back, score and fold folding line along lid. Apply glue above folding line and join card front and back together.

Tea Table Invitation

Materials

For one 4³⁄₁₆″ × 5″ (10.6 cm × 12.7 cm) invitation

Small teapot pattern on page 89

Equipment in work box, pages 4–6

3″ (7.7 cm) square of sturdy paper for teapot

5″ (12.7 cm) square of sturdy paper for tablecloth

5″ (12.7 cm) diameter scrap of lace paper doily

Heart-shaped paper punch, ½″ (1.3 cm) diameter for teabags, optional

3″ (7.7 cm) length of string, optional

Envelope, 4¼″ × 5⅛″ (10.8 cm × 13.0 cm), or Envelope C pattern, page 83, and instructions, pages 80–83

Instructions

1. Trace or photocopy small teapot pattern. Use needle or pin to pierce straight line of lid and curved side lines of spout and handle. Cut out pattern.
2. Hold pattern against 3″ (7.7 cm) paper scrap and draw around it, lightly transferring dots with sharp pencil tip. Cut out teapot. Use pen or pencil to draw lines at lid, spout, and handle.
3. If you wish to add teabags use paper punch to cut out four heart shapes. Sandwich string ends between two glued hearts. Use needle to pierce hole in teapot along lid line. Pull string through hole, adjust length, and tape string to back of teapot.
4. To make tablecloth, score and fold in half 5″ (12.7 cm) paper square. Unfold square and mark 1¼″ (3.2 cm) pencil line precisely on folding line. Cut 1¼″ (3.2 cm) slot in folding line. Refold card.
5. Trim and glue doily on card front to make tablecloth overlay. Lace can be one portion of doily or composite of several different sections. Place glue on front of tab along teapot base. Insert tab in card slot and press it against reverse side of card front.

Duckling Designs

For birth announcements, gift tags, place cards, or just for fun, these little ducklings are very easy to cut and color. For a pretty present tuck a duckling gift tag into waves created with scraps of jumbo rickrack or cut from paper with decorative edge scissors.

Duckling Note Card

Materials

For one 2¾″ × 3½″ (6.9 cm × 8.9 cm) card

Large pattern on page 89

Equipment in work box, pages 4–6

4″ × 6½″ (10.2 cm × 16.5 cm) piece of sturdy yellow paper

Paper punch, 3⁄16″ (0.5 cm) diameter

Orange and fine-line blue felt-tip pens

Envelope, 4¼″ × 5⅛″ (10.8 cm × 13.0 cm), or Envelope C pattern, page 83, and instructions, pages 80–83

Instructions

1. Photocopy or trace pattern and cut out. Use paper punch to cut out eye.
2. Score and fold paper in half crosswise to make 3¼″ × 4″ (8.2 cm × 10.2 cm) card.
3. Align "place on fold" edge of pattern with folded edge of card and straight bottom edge of pattern with lower edge of card. Hold pattern in place with tape or paper clips. Draw around shape and within eye. Remove pattern.
4. Anchor folded card layers together with clips. Use craft knife on protected work surface to cut out duckling shape. Cut wing lines indicated with solid lines on pattern. If desired, use pen to add color to beak and eye on all card surfaces.

Duckling Gift Tag

Instructions

1. Photocopy or trace pattern without bottom flap and cut out. Use paper punch to cut out eye.
2. Score and fold paper in half crosswise to make 2⅜″ × 3″ (6.0 cm × 7.7 cm) gift tag.
3. Complete steps 3 and 4 of Duckling Note Card instructions on page 24.

Materials

For one 2⅛″ × 2¾″ (5.4 cm × 6.9 cm) gift tag

Small pattern on page 89

Equipment in work box, pages 4–6

3″ × 4¾″ (7.7 cm × 12.0 cm) piece of yellow paper

Paper punch, ⅛″ (0.3 cm) diameter

Orange and fine-line blue felt-tip pens

Duckling Place Card

Instructions

1. Photocopy or trace pattern with bottom flap and cut out. Use paper punch to cut out eye.
2. Hold pattern in place on paper with tape or paper clips. Draw around shape and within eye. Remove pattern.
3. Use craft knife on protected work surface to cut out duckling shape. Cut wing lines, indicated with solid lines on pattern. If desired, use pens to add color to eyes and beak on all card surfaces. Score and fold back tab on line indicated on pattern.

Materials

For one 2⅛″ × 2¾″ (5.4 cm × 6.9 cm) place card

Small pattern on page 89

Equipment in work box, pages 4–6

2½″ × 3½″ (6.4 cm × 8.9 cm) piece of sturdy yellow paper

Paper punch, ⅛″ (0.3 cm) diameter

Orange and fine-line blue felt-tip pens

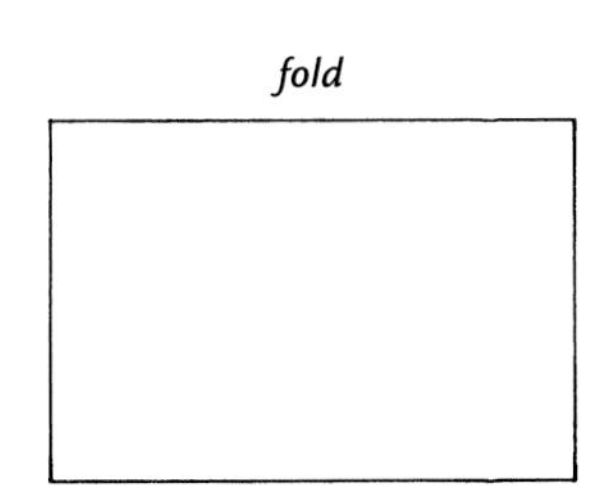

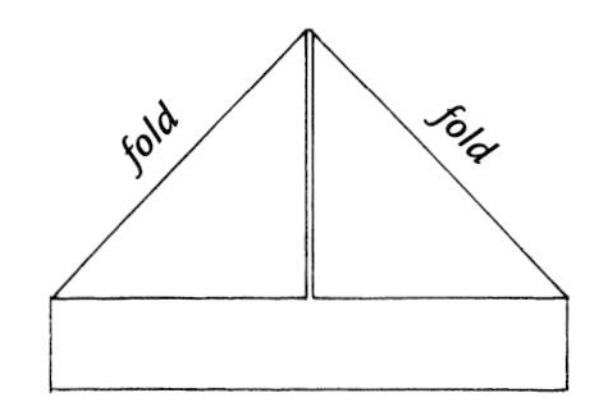

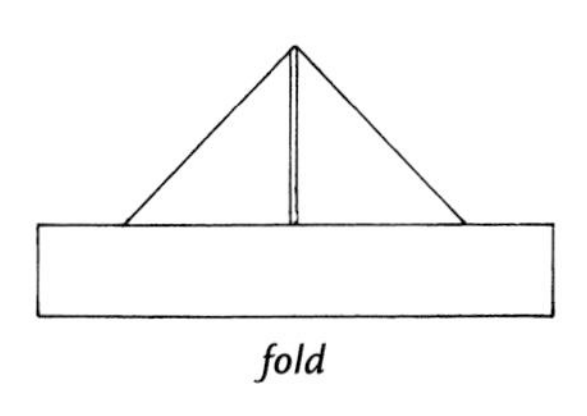

Use the drawings to make optional little hats for Ducklings-in-a-Row Card (next page). Fold 1⅞″ × 2½″ (4.8 cm × 6.4 cm) piece of paper for small hat. Fold 2⅜″ × 3⅜″ (6.0 cm × 8.5 cm) piece for larger hat.

Ducklings-in-a-Row Card

Materials

For one 2⅝″ × 12¾″ (6.7 cm × 32.4 cm) unfolded card

Small pattern on page 89

Equipment in work box, pages 4–6

3″ × 12¾″ (7.7 cm × 32.4 cm) piece of lightweight yellow paper

7″ (17.8 cm) square of origami paper for standing sailboat, optional

Envelope, 4¼″ × 5⅛″ (10.8 cm × 13.0 cm), or Envelope C pattern, page 83, and instructions, pages 80–83

Note: If paper does not fold well it may be necessary to score it before folding.

Instructions

1. Photocopy or trace pattern and cut out. Use paper punch to cut out eye.
2. Use pencil to mark both 12¾″ (32.4 cm) edges of paper at 2⅛″ (5.4 cm) intervals. Make accordion folds at all marked intervals, creasing folding lines sharply.
3. Place duckling pattern on folded paper. Align front and back edges of duckling with folded edges of paper and straight bottom edge of pattern with lower edge of paper. Hold pattern in place with paper clips. Draw around shape and within eye. Remove pattern.
4. Anchor folded edges of paper together with clips. Use craft knife on protected surface to cut out duckling shape. Cut wing lines, indicated with solid lines on pattern. If desired, use pen to add color to beak and eye on all card surfaces.

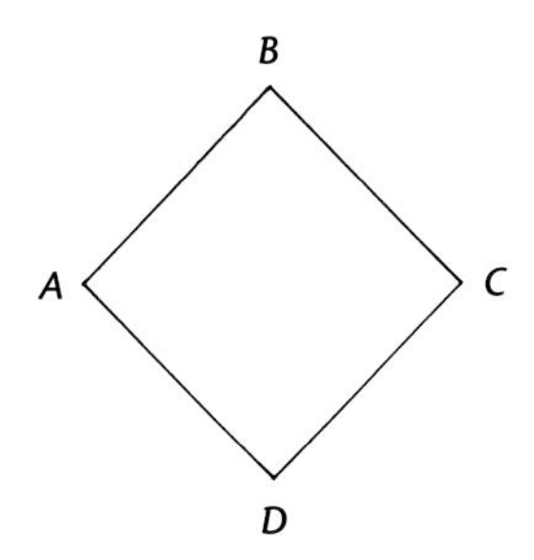

1. To make sailboat, lightly label corners of paper A, B, C, and D.

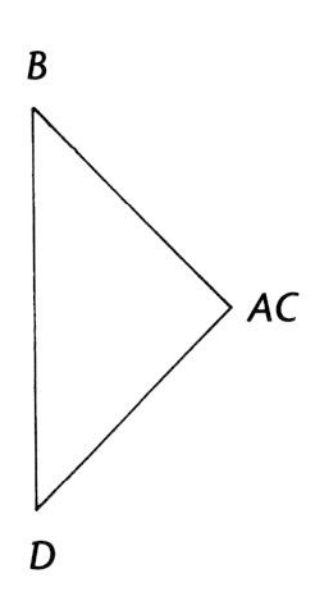

2. Fold paper in half diagonally, bringing corner A to corner C.

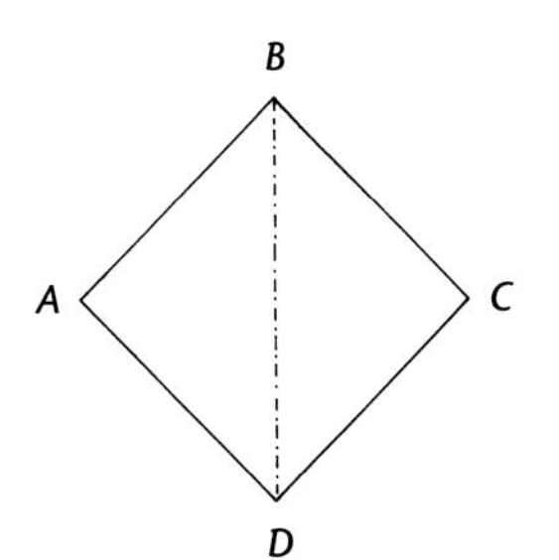

3. Unfold.

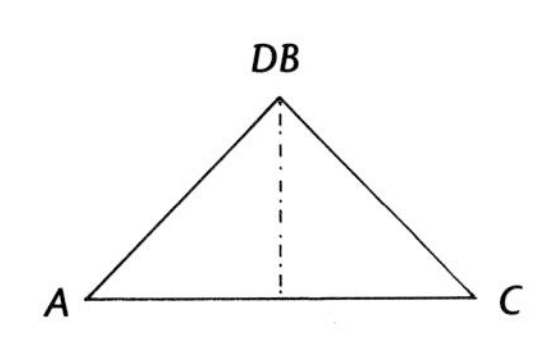

4. Fold paper in half diagonally, bringing corner D to corner B.

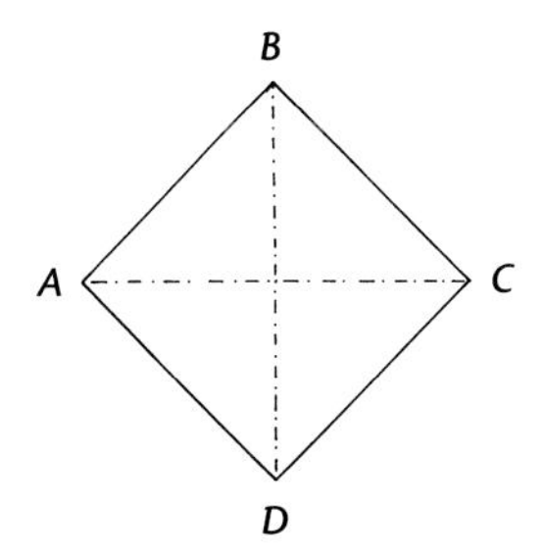

5. Unfold.

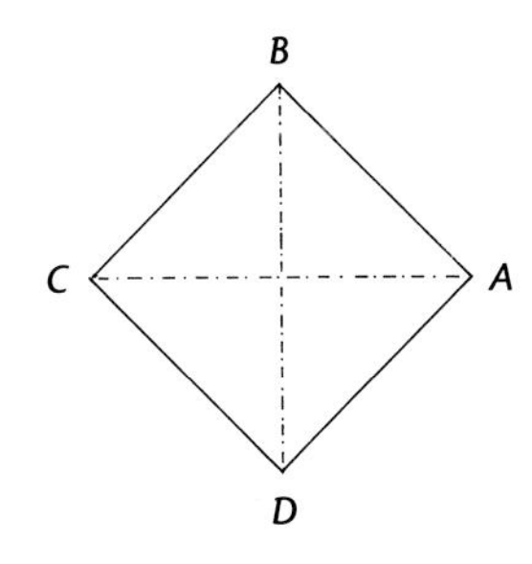

6. Flip to reverse side.

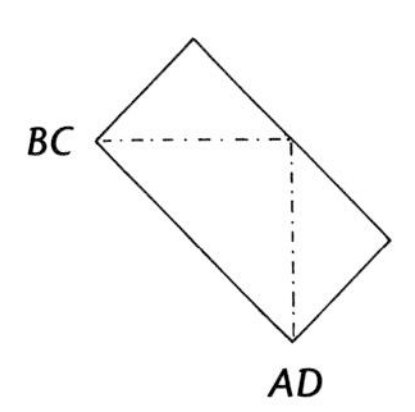

7. Fold unit, bringing corner B to corner C and corner A to corner D.

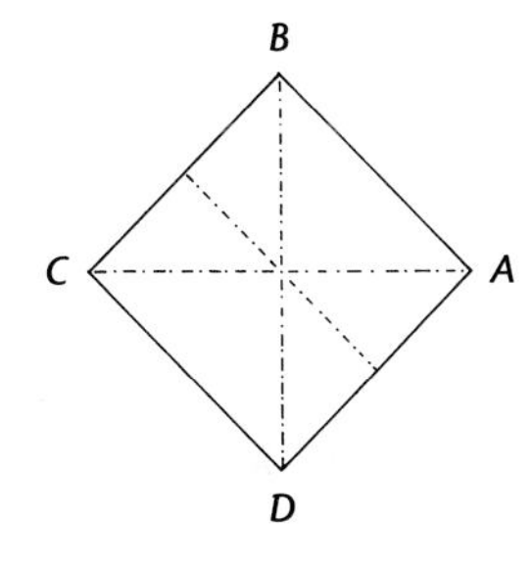

8. Unfold.

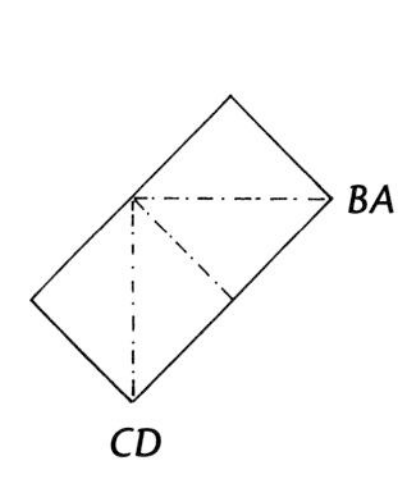

9. Fold unit, bringing corner C to corner D and corner B to corner A.

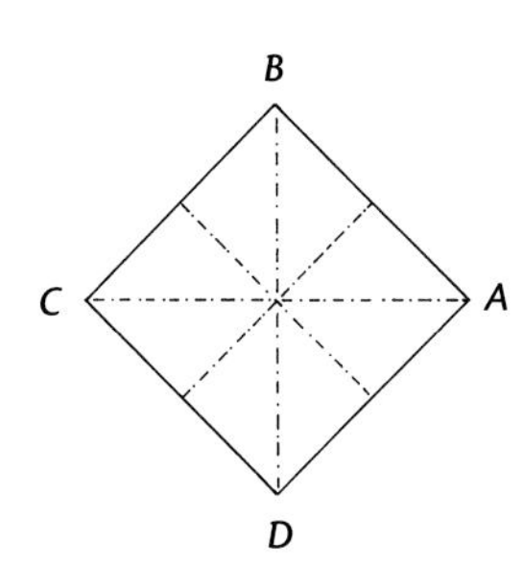

10. Unfold.

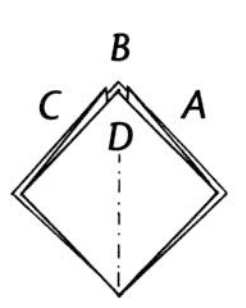

11. Fold corner D up to meet corner B, collapsing creases and pushing corners C and A inside unit so corners C, B, and A meet together under corner D at top.

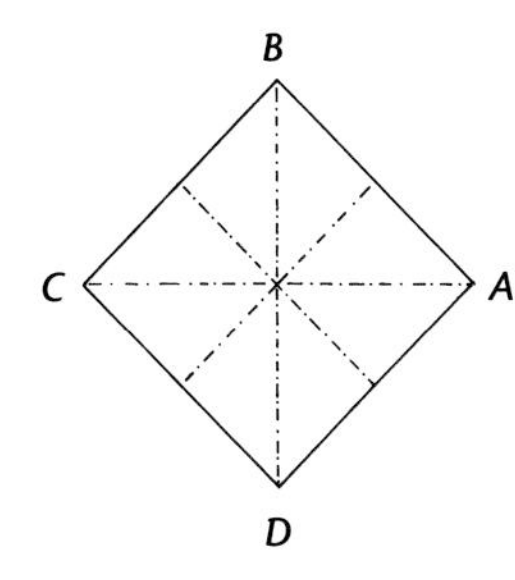

12. Unfold.

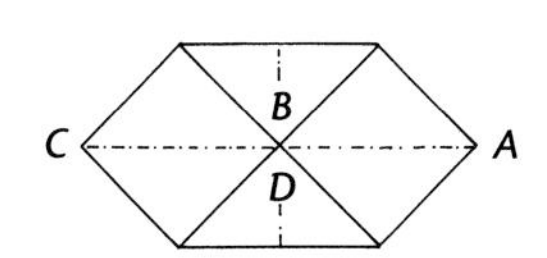

13. Fold corners B and D so they meet at center of square.

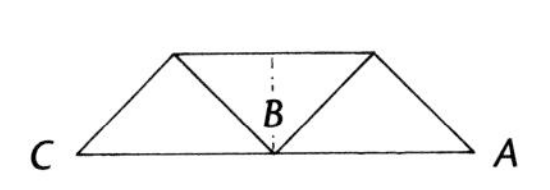

14. Crease unit along folding line CA.

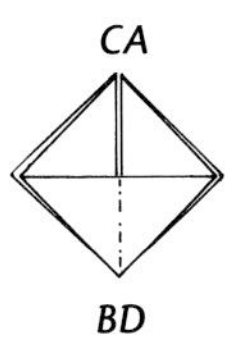

15. Collapse folding line CA, pushing corners C and A up inside unit so they meet at center top.

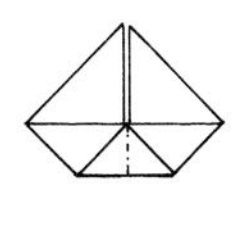

16. Fold up center bottom point of boat to make prop.

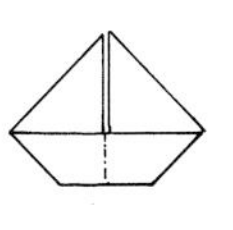

17. Flip to reverse side.

Baby Bib Announcement

The paper lace and satin ribbon embellishing this baby bib card suggest the heirloom look of embroidered linen. These French lace doilies were purchased at a national greeting card retailer, so perhaps you will be able to find the same ones. If you must use a different doily design, for best results select one that has a rather closed center area. Then if necessary, add or subtract a little around the outside edge of the bib circle in order to make the pattern and the doily shape compatible. If you make the envelope too, use an additional doily to line it.

Materials

For one 4″ (10.2 cm) announcement

- Pattern on page 90
- Equipment in work box, pages 4–6
- 5″ (12.7 cm) square of tracing paper
- 4″ × 7½″ (10.2 cm × 19.1 cm) piece of sturdy pastel paper
- 4″ (10.2 cm) diameter lace paper doily
- 15″ (38.1 cm) length of narrow satin ribbon
- Envelope, 4¼″ × 5⅛″ (10.8 cm × 13.0 cm), or Envelope C pattern, page 83, and instructions, pages 80–83

Instructions

1. Trace bib pattern and cut out.
2. Using craft knife and straightedge on protected work surface, score and fold pastel paper in half crosswise. Align "place on fold" edge of pattern along folded edge of paper. Anchor with tape or clips and draw around shape. Cut out.
3. Find best placement and center bib pattern on back of doily. Trace within neck opening. Remove pattern and cut bib neck with scissors (not craft knife, because knife blade might tear doily).
4. Cut ribbon in half. Glue in place on paper bib neck edge. Apply glue to paper bib front and press doily in place on it.

Bassinet Card

Welcome a new baby or celebrate a christening with this cozy greeting. Its cuteness just might make it a candidate for inclusion in the newcomer's baby keepsake album.

Instructions

1. Trace or photocopy patterns. Glue them to acetate if you wish. Cut out.
2. Score and fold sturdy white paper in half crosswise.
3. Tape or clip "place on fold" edge of bassinet pattern to folded edge of white paper. Trace around pattern and remove it. Using craft knife on protected work surface, cut out bassinet and reserve.
4. On white bond paper, mark ruffle pattern and all folding lines. Remove pattern. Score sixteen lines indicated. Refer to drawing to fold pleats. Open pleats. Place glue at each dot on ruffle top edge where indicated on pattern. Pleat again and hold in place until dry. Spread thin line of glue on tabs A and B and along top and bottom edges of ruffle. Place pleated ruffle on bassinet, aligning left and right edges carefully. Hold in place until dry or press under heavy book.
5. Glue pastel paper strip to top of ruffle. Trim to fit. Glue remaining piece to hood of bassinet and trim to fit.
6. On tan paper mark one bear. Draw eyes. Cut out bear and slip arms over bassinet side. Add glue to bear if you wish. To add tail, use paper punch to make small circle and glue in place.

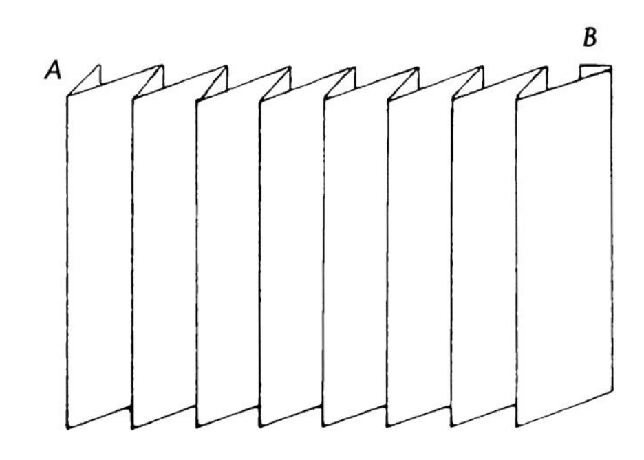

Pleat ruffle, fold tabs A and B behind pleats, and glue to bassinet.

Materials

For one 3⅞″ × 4″ (9.8 cm × 10.2 cm) square card

Patterns on page 90

Equipment in work box, pages 4-6

4¼″ × 9″ (10.8 cm × 22.8 cm) piece of sturdy white paper

3″ × 8½″ (7.7 cm × 21.6 cm) piece of white bond paper

¼″ × 6″ (0.6 cm × 15.2 cm) piece of pastel paper

2″ × 2½″ (5.1 cm × 6.4 cm) piece of tan paper

Envelope, 4⅛″ × 5½″ (10.5 cm × 14.0 cm), or Envelope A pattern, page 82, and instructions, pages 80-82

Animal Note Cards and Gift Tags

Materials

For one 3⅜ × 5¾" (8.5 cm × 14.6 cm) elephant or 3½" × 6¼" (8.9 cm × 15.9 cm) alligator

Patterns on page 91

Equipment in work box, pages 4-6

4" × 13" (10.2 cm × 33.0 cm) piece of sturdy paper for animal body

2¾" × 4" (6.9 cm × 10.2 cm) additional piece of paper for elephant ears

Paper punch, ⅛" (0.3 cm) diameter

Envelope, 3⅝" × 6½" (9.2 cm × 16.5 cm), or Envelope D pattern, page 83, and instructions, pages 80-83

Materials

For one 1⅞" × 3¼" (4.8 cm × 8.2 cm) elephant or one 2" × 3½" (5.1 cm × 8.9 cm) alligator

Patterns on page 92

Equipment in work box, pages 4-6

2½" × 9" (6.4 cm × 22.8 cm) piece of paper

Scraps of wallpaper rescued from a discontinued sample book were used to make these animal notes, but any sturdy paper will do. Smaller patterns are provided so you can make gift tags too.

Elephant or Alligator Note Cards

Instructions

1. Trace or photocopy patterns and cut out. Use paper punch to cut eye.
2. Using craft knife and straightedge on protected work surface, score and fold paper in half crosswise. Align "place on fold" edge of pattern with folded edge of paper. Anchor with masking tape or paper clips. Draw around shape and mark eye. Cut out animal using paper punch for eye. If making elephant, place ear pattern on paper and trace two. Transfer folding line and cut out ears. Score folding line and crease. Apply glue to tab on each ear and glue one in place on card front and one on card back.

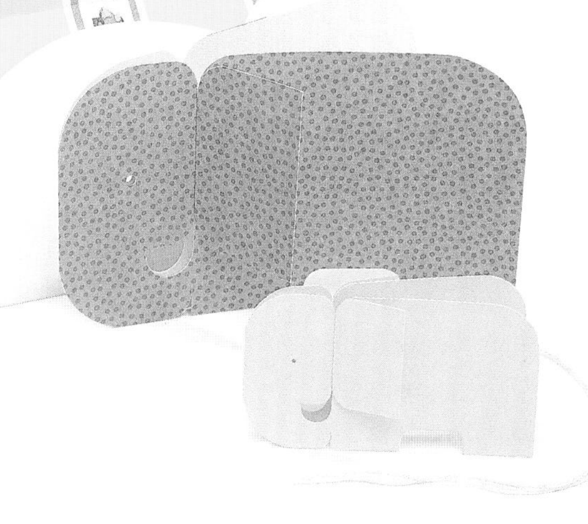

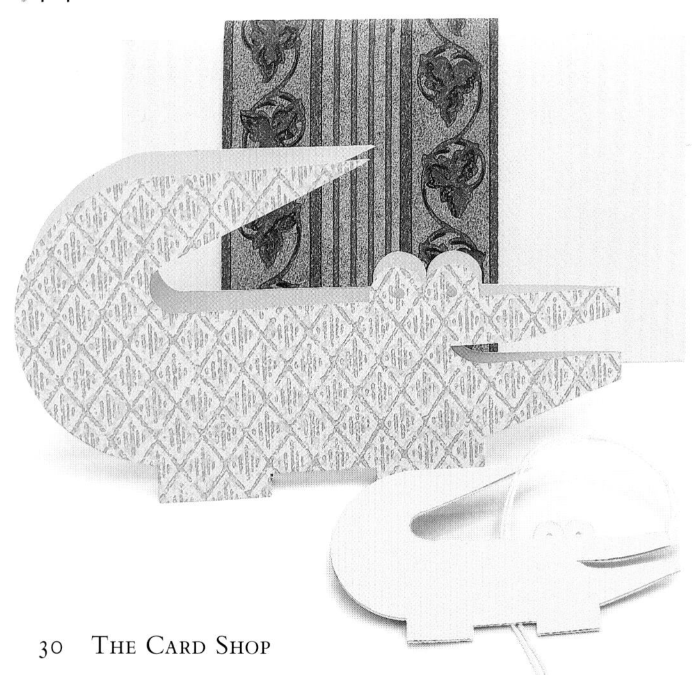

Animal Gift Tags

Instructions

Refer to preceding instructions for animal note cards, using large needle instead of paper punch for eyes.

Piggy Bank Note

This little piggy holds a money present, a gift certificate, or tickets for a special event. Fold-up pockets are glued inside the note to make sure that the surprise won't get lost inside the envelope.

Materials

For one 4½″ × 4³⁄₁₆″ (11.4 cm × 10.6 cm) note

Patterns on page 92

Equipment in work box, pages 4–6

6″ × 8″ (15.2 cm × 20.4 cm) piece of sturdy, patterned pink paper, scored and folded in half to make 3″ × 4″ (7.7 cm × 10.2 cm) note

Scraps of pink paper or pink felt-tip pen for cheeks

Dark fine-line pen for eyes

Envelope, 4¼″ × 5⅛″ (10.8 cm × 13.0 cm), or Envelope C pattern, page 83, and instructions, pages 80–83

Instructions

1. Photocopy or trace large pig with pocket and ear patterns and cut out. To make template of pig pattern, cut out mouth, top slot, small area between legs, and circles for eye and cheek. Use pin to pierce ear placement line and pocket folding line.
2. Align "place on fold" nose edge of pig pattern with folded edge of card, holding pattern in place with removable tape or paper clips. Draw around shape and within mouth, top slot, small area between legs, and circles for eye and nose. Push pencil point into pattern pinholes to transfer ear placement line and pocket folding line. To make ears, align "place on fold" edge of ear pattern with folded edge of card paper and trace around shape. Draw another ear in the same manner. Remove patterns.
3. Secure folded card layers together with paper clips. Use craft knife on protected work surface to cut out pig with pocket and ears. Cut out mouth line and small area between legs. Score pocket folding line. Hold pig with pocket pattern against card back and mark ear placement line, pocket folding line, and circles for eye and cheek.
4. With inside of opened card facing you, spread glue on pocket portion of each pig within glue area indicated by dots on pattern. Fold up each pocket and glue to inside of card. Allow to dry. Glue folded ears onto inside and outside surfaces of card.

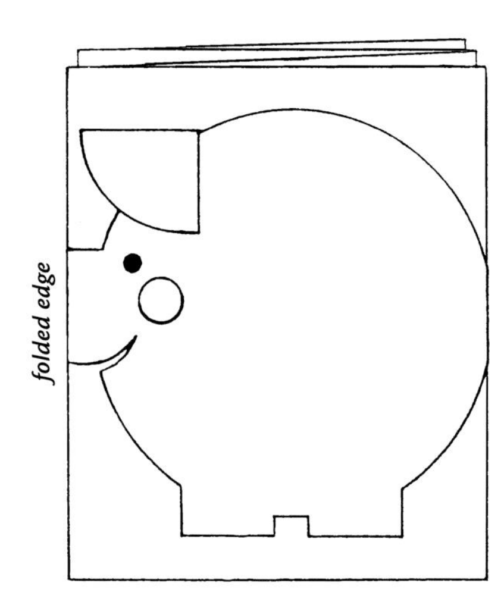

Place small pig pattern on accordion-folded paper.

5. Use felt-tip pen to draw eyes on front and back of card. For cheeks, cut out ⅜″ (1.0 cm) diameter circles and glue in place on card. Or, cheeks can be colored with felt-tip pen.
6. To make baby garland for piggy back card, trace small pig pattern. Make template by cutting out cheek, eye, and mouth and use pin to pierce ear line. Fold 2¼″ × 7½″ (5.7 cm × 19.1 cm) piece of paper in half crosswise and unfold. Bring each 2¼″ (5.7 cm) cut edge of paper to meet at center folding line and crease. Unfold paper and then accordion-fold it on existing folding lines. Unit should resemble drawing with right side of paper showing on front. Place small pig pattern on folded unit, aligning nose edge with folding line. Draw around shape, transferring details. Hold paper layers together with tape or clips. Cut out pig shape. Unfold garland. Hold pattern against each pig and transfer details. Use felt-tip pens to draw eyes and cheeks. Define ears with pencil lines.

3

Summer Wishes

Sailboat Card

You can lift these little folded sailboats out of the waves to stage your own regatta. The card is very easy to make, but when you fold the water area be sure to clearly label the glue tabs so you won't inadvertently glue the water in place upside down.

Materials

For one 4¼″ × 5½″ (10.8 cm × 14.0 cm) card

Patterns on page 93

Equipment in work box, pages 4–6

Erasable transfer paper

4¼″ × 11″ (10.8 cm × 28.0 cm) piece of sturdy blue paper, scored and folded in half crosswise

6″ × 7″ (15.2 cm × 17.8 cm) piece of dark blue origami or bond paper

Five 1½″ (3.8 cm) squares of origami paper

Envelope, 4⅜″ × 5¾″ (11.1 cm × 14.6 cm), or Envelope B pattern, page 82, and instructions, pages 80–82

Instructions

1. Photocopy or trace patterns with markings and cut out. Tape or clip card pattern to folded paper. Slide transfer paper between layers and draw on top of pattern to transfer glue areas and placement lines.
2. Tape or clip water pattern to blue surface of origami paper. Slide transfer paper between layers and draw on top of pattern to transfer outline, glue tabs, and folding lines. Remove pattern.
3. Cut water to size of pattern. Score all folding lines on colored side of paper. As you fold water piece, refer to pattern and note that each folding line is marked with V to indicate valley fold or M to indicate mountain fold. Refer to drawing at top right of page 35 and fold edges of water piece to resemble it.
4. Again referring to drawing at at top right of page 35, start at top of water piece and apply glue to both folded side edges (directions follow). Note narrow glue margins on side edges of pattern. Until you get down to tab B at bottom edge, glue should only be applied to front and back of each pocket area. As you work use clips to hold glued edges together until dry. Pockets fold behind tiers. Glue pocket 1 to tab A and back of tier 1. Glue pocket 2 to front

of tier 1 and back of tier 2. Glue pocket 3 to front of tier 2 and back of tier 3. Glue pocket 4 to front of tier 3 and back of tier 4. Glue pocket 5 to front of tier 4 and back of tier 5. Fold tab B to back of unit. It will overlap lower edge of pocket 5. Glue tab B to back of tier 5 and back of pocket 5.

5. Place glue on entire tab A, entire tab B, and in narrow margin along each cut edge of water piece. Place water piece on card. Be sure glue from tab A does not close pocket 1 and glue on other water edges does not close card. Place clips on edges until glue is dry.
6. Fold sailboats, referring to Drawings 1 through 10. Insert boats in pockets.

pocket 1
← glue tab A
tier 1
pocket 2
tier 2
pocket 3
tier 3
pocket 4
tier 4
pocket 5
tier 5
← folding line
glue tab B
cut edge of tab B
Fold up tab B and glue it to back of tier 5 and pocket 5.

Fold and glue pockets of water piece on water edges.

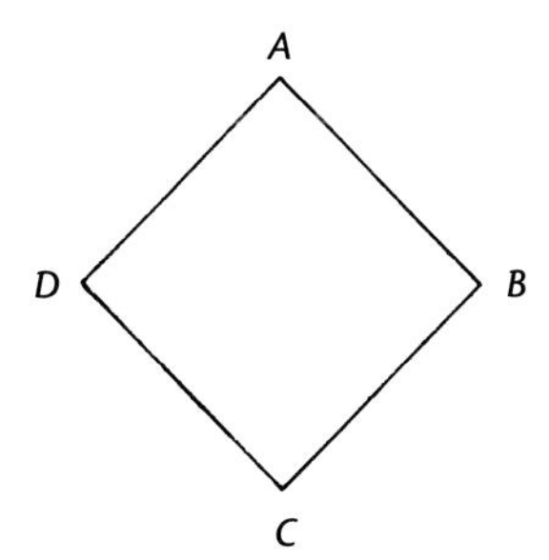

1. On work surface, place square on diagonal with color side facing you. Lightly label each corner of square.

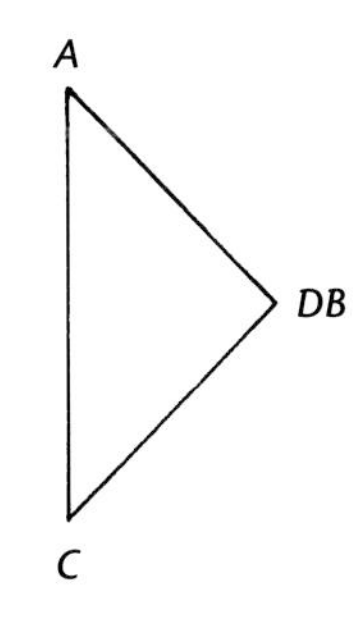

2. Bring corner D over to corner B to make vertical fold AC through center. White surface of paper will face you.

A
D
B
C

3. Open fold.

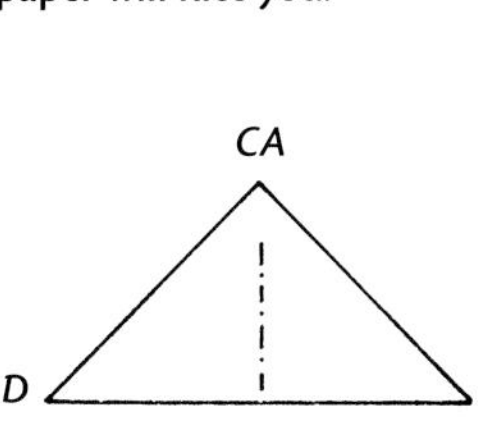

4. Bring corner C up to meet corner A to make horizontal fold DB through center.

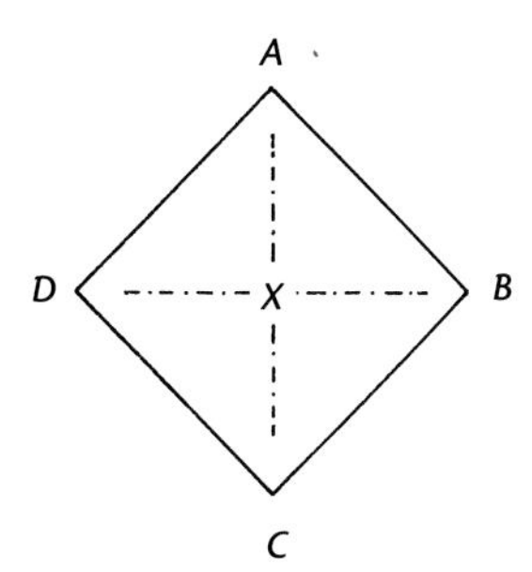

5. Open fold. Place X at center of square where folding lines cross each other.

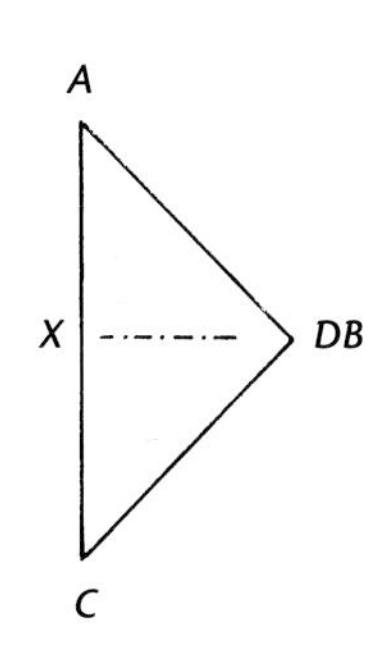

6. Again crease on vertical folding line AC bringing corner D to corner B so white surface faces you.

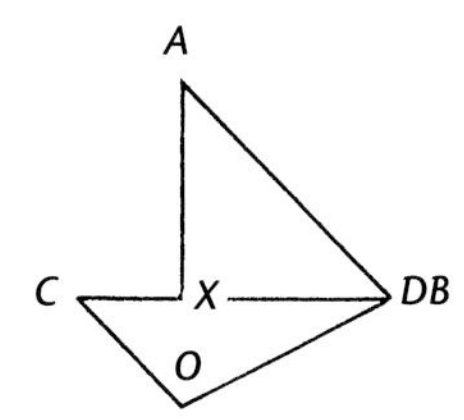

7. Keeping edges CB and underlying edge BC together, fold them up to front so edges align with folding line XD.

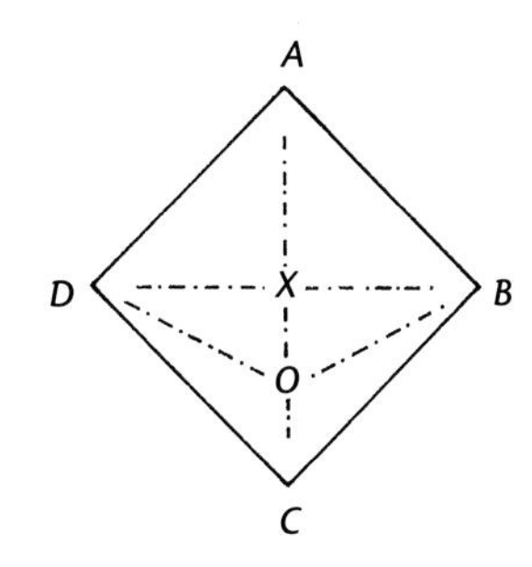

8. Open all folds so square is flat and color surface faces you again.

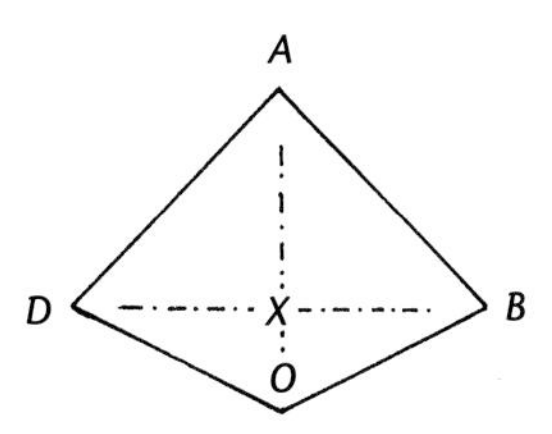

9. Push corner C away from you so unit folds on lines DO and OB.

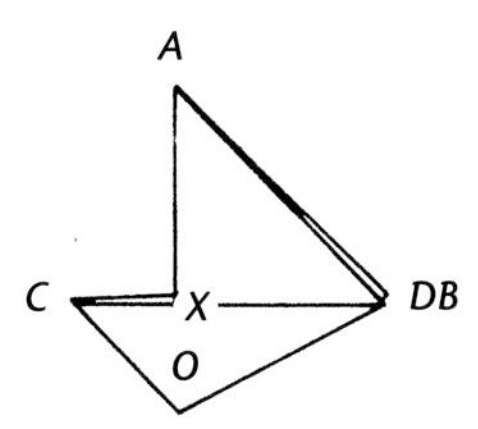

10. Close unit like covers of a book, bringing corner D to corner B and creasing on vertical folding line AO. Insert boat in pocket.

Pinwheel Card

Beach-ball-bright colors were used to make this set of playful note cards. Each one is constructed from a single piece of duplex paper that is cut and folded to resemble a pinwheel.

Materials

For one 4″ (10.2 cm) square card

Pattern on page 94

Equipment in work box, pages 4–6

4″ × 8″ (10.2 cm × 20.4 cm) piece of erasable transfer paper

4″ × 8″ (10.2 cm × 20.4 cm) piece of sturdy paper

Scrap of paper for center dots

Paper punch, ½″ (1.3 cm) diameter, or circle pattern included

Envelope, 4¼″ × 5⅛″ (10.8 cm × 13.0 cm), or Envelope C pattern, page 83, and instructions, pages 80–83

Instructions

1. Trace or photocopy pattern and cut it out. If pattern has been photocopied, trim precisely to 4″ × 8″ (10.2 cm × 20.4 cm) edges.
2. On protected work surface, stack papers in following order: pinwheel paper, surface for inside of card facing up; transfer paper, transfer surface down; pattern, right-side up. Tape each layer separately to work surface. Use pencil to draw over all pattern lines. Pierce center dots with pin. Remove pattern and transfer paper.
3. Referring to Drawing 1, use craft knife on protected work surface to score all broken lines and cut all solid lines. This is inside surface of card.
4. Referring to Drawing 2, flip paper over to reverse side. This is outside surface of card.
5. Referring to Drawing 3, fold tips of pinwheel blades to each center dot and glue in place. Cover center of each pinwheel with colored paper dot. Fold card on center folding line.

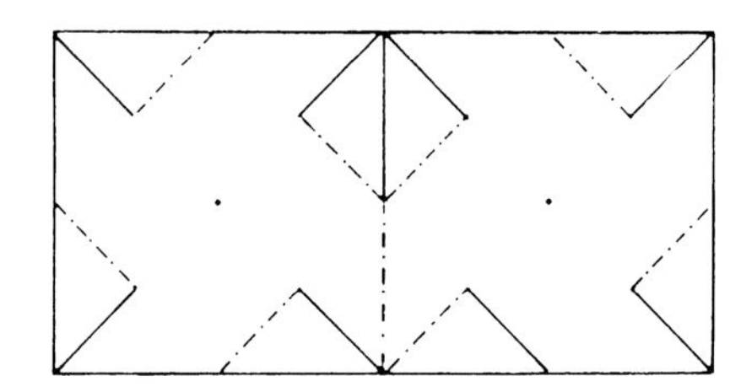

1. Score and cut paper on inside of card.

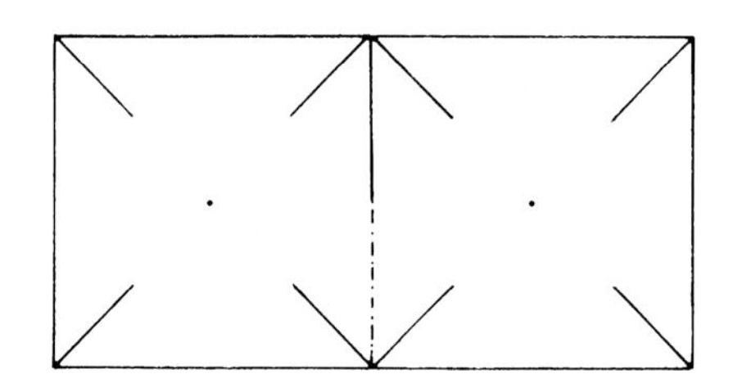

2. Turn paper over to outside of card.

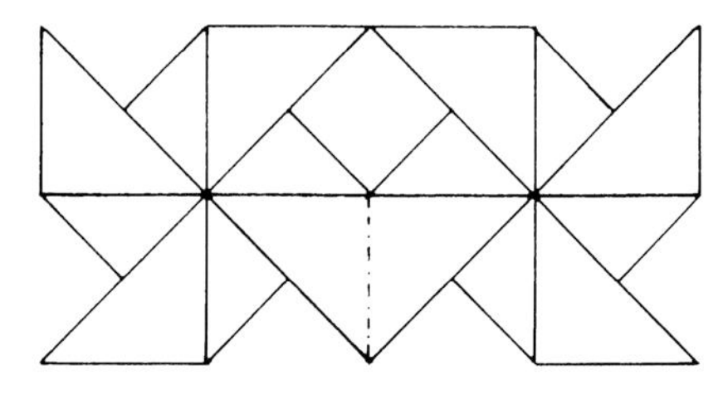

3. Fold blade tips to center dots.

Tomato Pincushion Note

The prosaic contents of a sewing basket become playful symbols of creativity when enlarged beyond their usual proportions. This jumbo pincushion opens to offer space for a message, as does the strawberry tethered to it.

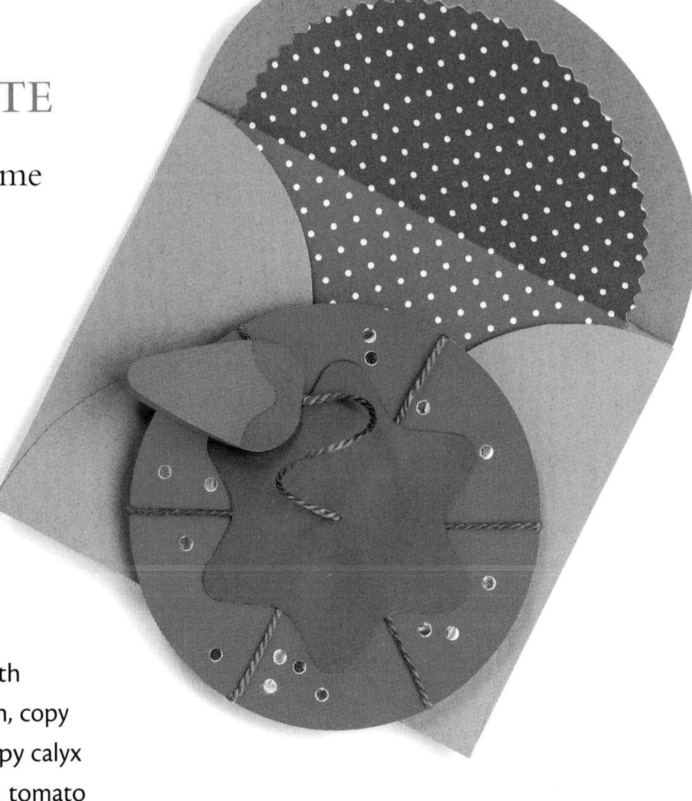

Instructions

1. Trace or photocopy patterns for tomato, strawberry, and both calyxes. Glue them to acetate if you wish. On tomato pattern, copy straight segment lines and large dots. There is no need to copy calyx placement. Pierce pattern with pin to mark these details. On tomato calyx and strawberry calyx, copy and pierce center dot.
2. Cut red paper into two $4\frac{1}{2}$″ (11.4 cm) squares, reserving leftover scrap. Draw tomato shaped pincushion on one square, transferring segment lines with pencil pushed into pinholes on pattern. Tape this paper, right-side up, on second square of red paper. Cut out tomato shaped pincushion on outline, resulting in two circles. On unmarked circle (card back), use craft knife to score folding line across center. Fold circle in half and set aside.
3. Working on perimeter of marked circle (card front), use fingernail to make very tiny notch where each segment line touches edge of shape. To define segments of pincushion, use following method to wrap string or ribbon around circle: tape one end of one string at A; guide string into notch on edge; lead string across center of reverse side of circle; guide string into notch on opposite edge; bring string end to opposite A; and tape it there. Repeat process with two of three remaining pieces of string, leading one string from B to B and another string from C to C so tomato will have six segments. Set piece aside.
4. On green paper draw one tomato calyx, transferring and piercing dot at center. Thread remaining piece of string or ribbon into large-eyed needle and pass needle through calyx center hole from front to back. Remove thread end from needle's eye. Tape end of thread on reverse side of calyx. Referring to photograph, glue calyx in place at center of tomato.

Materials

For one $3\frac{15}{16}$″ (10.0 cm) diameter pincushion card

Patterns on page 95

Equipment in work box, pages 4-6

$4\frac{1}{2}$″ × 10″ (11.4 cm × 25.4 cm) piece of sturdy red paper

$3\frac{1}{4}$″ × $4\frac{1}{4}$″ (8.2 cm × 10.8 cm) piece of green paper

Small scrap of metallic silver paper for pins, optional

Paper punch, $\frac{1}{8}$″ (0.3 cm) diameter for pins, optional

Four 7″ (17.8 cm) lengths of green string, pearl cotton, embroidery thread, or very narrow ribbon

Large-eyed needle

Envelope, $4\frac{1}{4}$″ × $5\frac{1}{8}$″ (10.8 cm × 13.0 cm), or Envelope C pattern, page 83, and instructions, pages 80-83

5. On reserved card back, spread glue above folding line. Place this glue-covered area on reverse side of card front, aligning folding line of card back with one of strings on reverse side of card front. Allow to dry.
6. To make strawberry, cut 1½″ × 4″ (3.8 cm × 10.2 cm) piece from red paper scrap. Score and fold in half crosswise to make 1½″ × 2″ (3.8 cm × 5.1 cm) piece. Align "place on fold" edge of strawberry with folded edge of red paper. Trace around edge, remove pattern, and cut out berry. Set aside.
7. To make strawberry calyx, cut 1½″ × 3″ (3.8 cm × 7.7 cm) piece of paper from green scrap. Score and fold in half crosswise to make square piece. Align "place on fold" edge of calyx pattern with folded edge of paper. Trace around edge, remove pattern, and cut out calyx. Set aside.
8. At center of tomato, trim thread emerging from calyx to 4″ (10.2 cm). Thread end of string into large-eyed needle and pass needle through hole at center of strawberry calyx. Remove needle and trim another ½″ (1.3 cm) off of thread end. Leave about ¼″ (0.6 cm) of thread inside calyx and tape end in place. Fold calyx over strawberry top and glue in place.
9. If you wish, use paper punch to make silver pinheads and glue them in place randomly on pincushion.

PAINTBRUSH NOTE CARD

The familiar, pleasing shape of an ordinary paintbrush makes a cute yet simple card for many occasions. Unfold a store-bought, business-size envelope and use it as a pattern to make a complementary custom envelope for the card.

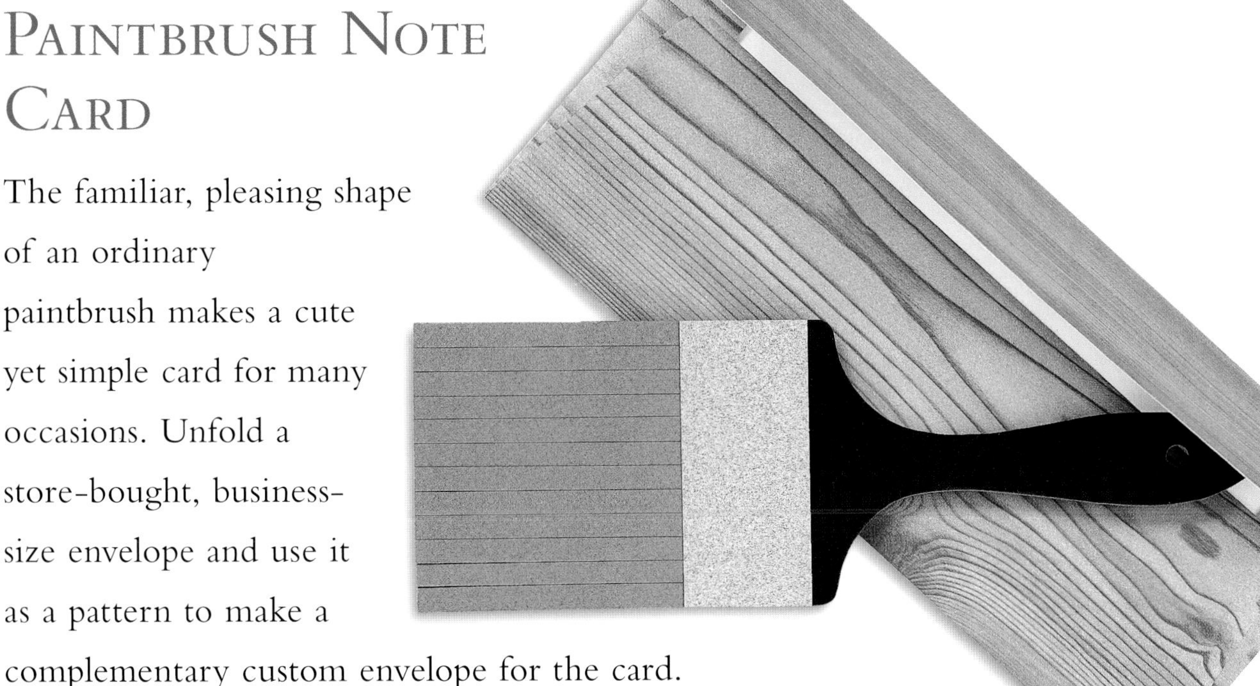

Instructions

1. Photocopy or trace pattern, transferring placement lines and cutting lines. Cut out pattern. Punch out hole. Use pin to pierce bristle cutting lines at top.
2. Score and fold tan paper in half lengthwise. Referring to drawing, glue black and gray paper or foil in place.
3. Set "place on fold" edge of pattern on folded edge of prepared paper, aligning dotted lines on pattern with gray or foil band on paper. Hold in place with clips or tape. Trace around pattern and mark bristle lines at top and bottom. Remove pattern but leave clips in place.
4. Using craft knife on protected surface, cut out paintbrush but not bristles. Punch out hole in handle. Open card so it is flat and cut between bristles (including one resting on fold line) on card front only.

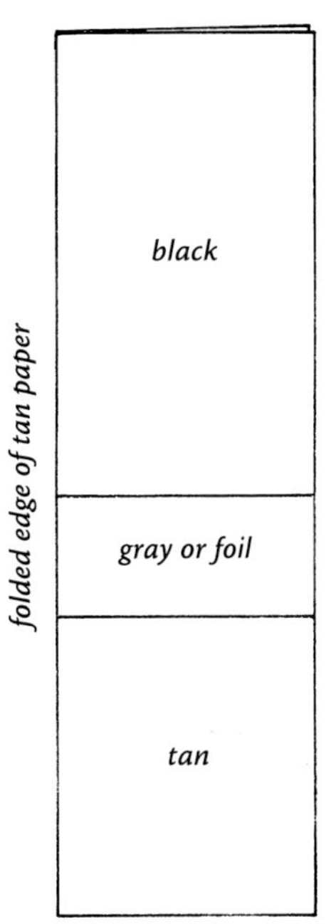

Glue papers together.

Materials

For one 3" × 9⅜" (7.7 cm × 23.8 cm) note card

Pattern on page 95

Equipment in work box, pages 4–6

6" × 10" (15.2 cm × 25.4 cm) piece of sturdy tan paper

1⅜" × 3" (3.5 cm × 7.7 cm) piece of gray or metallic foil paper

3" × 5¼" (7.7 cm × 13.3 cm) piece of black paper

Paper punch, ¼" (0.6 cm) diameter

Envelope, 4⅛" × 9½" (10.5 cm × 24.1 cm)

Materials

For one 2⅞″ × 9⅛″ (7.3 cm × 23.2 cm) note card

Patterns on page 96

Equipment in work box, pages 4–6

Two 3¼″ × 9½″ (8.2 cm × 24.1 cm) pieces of sturdy paper for fin piece

Two 2½″ × 8″ (6.4 cm × 20.3 cm) pieces of sturdy paper for fish

Envelope, 4⅛″ × 9½″ (10.5 cm × 24.1 cm)

Note: Unfold a store-bought envelope and use it as a pattern for creating your own unique envelope if you wish.

Fish Note Card

Inspired by an antique New England weather vane, this fish note card is very easy to make. Add a touch of whimsy by mailing the fish with a few strands of green or blue shredded paper inside a glassine or vellum envelope to suggest an aquarium.

Instructions

1. Trace or photocopy patterns. Cut out patterns and details.
2. Tape or clip fin pattern onto one piece of fin paper. Draw around shape and remove pattern. Before cutting, tape or clip marked paper to remaining fin paper. On protected work surface use craft knife to cut out fin piece and set aside.
3. Tape or clip fish pattern on one piece of fish paper. Draw around shape and remove pattern. Before cutting, tape or clip marked paper to remaining fish paper. Cut out fish shape as well as gill, mouth, and eye.
4. Glue one fish to each fin, making sure the fish swim in opposite directions. On wrong side of each fin piece, lightly score tail folding line and crease. Starting at score lines, glue tails together to make hinge.

Knife, Fork, and Spoon Invitation

Perfect for a picnic or a summer cookout, this invitation almost shouts, "Let's eat!" Party details such as time, place, and date are written horizontally inside this top-folded card.

Materials

For one 3″ × 6″ (7.7 cm × 15.2 cm) invitation

Pattern on page 96

Equipment in work box, pages 4–6

6½″ (16.5 cm) square of sturdy gray paper or very lightweight foil board

3¼″ (8.2 cm) square of colored paper

Paper punch, ¼″ (0.6 cm) diameter

Envelope, 3⅝″ × 6½″ (9.2 cm × 16.5 cm), or Envelope D pattern, page 83, and instructions, pages 80–83

Instructions

1. Photocopy or trace pattern, copy markings, and cut out.
2. Score and fold gray square in half to make card. With folded edge on left, place card on work surface. Glue colored paper to lower portion of card, aligning all edges. Set "place on fold" edge of pattern on folded edge of card. Align horizontal dotted pattern line with top edge of colored paper and use clips or tape to hold pattern in place. Draw around shape of utensils. Remove pattern but leave clips in place.
3. Use craft knife on protected surface to cut out shape. Use fine pencil lines to define lines between each utensil. Open invitation, turn it horizontally, and write party details on each utensil from end to end.

Hamburger Note Card

Circles and squares are the only ingredients for this quick and easy hamburger note card. Make it just the way you like it, holding the onion or adding more cheese, and then garnish it with your own special words of love and affection.

Materials

For one 4″ (10.2 cm) square note card

Patterns on pages 97-98

Equipment in work box, pages 4-6

Two 5″ × 10″ (12.7 cm × 25.4 cm) pieces of tan paper for bun, crust sides

Two 5″ × 10″ (12.7 cm × 25.4 cm) pieces of cream paper for bun, bread sides

Four 5″ (12.7 cm) squares of paper for lettuce, onion, cheese, and burger

Sesame-colored paper scrap for seeds, optional

Pencil or felt -tip pen for rings of onion

Scalloped paper edger scissors, optional

Paper punch, ⅛″ (0.3 cm) diameter for seeds, optional

Envelope, 4¼″ × 5⅛″ (10.8 cm × 13.0 cm), or Envelope C pattern, page 83, and instructions, pages 80-83

Instructions

1. Trace or photocopy patterns with markings. Make one additional pattern for bread portion of bun using dotted line just inside bun crust pattern line. Pierce pattern with pin to make tiny holes for tranferring placement and folding lines onto papers.
2. Use pattern to cut one tan bun crust. Also cut one slightly smaller cream bun piece for inside of bun. Center and glue cream bread piece on crust. Hold pattern against inside of bun and use sharp pencil on right-hand edge of pattern to transfer large dot and placement line. Do not score or fold bun.
3. Use pattern to cut one green lettuce leaf, using decorative edger if you wish. Hold pattern against right side of lettuce and transfer large dots and folding lines. Score right edge folding line on front of lettuce and score left edge folding line on back of lettuce. Crease folding lines, folding left edge glue tab to front of lettuce and right edge glue tab to back. Place bun on work surface, bread side up. Flip lettuce to reverse side with glue tab on right edge folded under lettuce. Place glue on right edge tab. Overlap bun with lettuce, aligning dot and folding line on right edge of folded lettuce glue tab with dot and placement line on right edge of bun bread side. Allow to dry.
4. Cut one onion slice and use compass to draw concentric circles on it. Use colored pencil or pen to draw onion rings. Hold pattern against onion and transfer large dots and folding lines. Score folding lines, folding right edge glue tab to front of onion and left edge glue tab to back. Leave burger unit in last position with reverse side of folded lettuce facing up. Unfold lettuce glue tab on left-hand edge. With right side of

onion slice facing up, apply glue to tab behind onion's left edge. Place onion right-side up on top of lettuce, matching large dots and aligning folding line of onion left edge glue tab with unfolded folding line of lettuce left edge glue tab. Allow to dry. Leaving unit in same position and working on same edge, apply glue to lettuce glue tab, fold it over onion, and allow to dry.

5. Trim yellow paper to make 3¾″ (9.5 cm) square for cheese. Flip cheese to reverse side. Draw very light pencil line across middle of square to help with alignment. Leave burger unit in last position with right side of folded onion facing up. Glue tab on onion's right edge should be folded over onion so it faces you. Place paper scrap under onion glue tab so it protects onion surface and spread glue on tab. Overlap onion with cheese slice, aligning cut edge of cheese with folded edge of onion glue tab on right-hand edge of unit. Remove protective paper scrap and allow to dry.
6. Cut one brown burger piece using decorative edge scissors if you wish. Hold pattern against burger, and use sharp pencil to transfer large dots and folding lines. Score folding lines, folding right glue tab to front of burger and left glue tab to back. Leave burger unit in last position with reverse side of cheese facing up. With right side of burger facing up, apply glue to left tab behind burger. Place burger right-side up on top of reverse side of cheese, aligning folded edge of left burger glue tab with cut edge of cheese on left-hand edge of unit. Allow to dry.
7. Cut one more tan bun crust and one cream piece for inside of bun. Hold pattern against bread side of bun and use pencil on left-hand edge of pattern to trace dot and placement line. Do not score or fold bun. Leave burger unit in last position with right side of hamburger facing up. Glue tab on right-hand edge of burger should be folded flat on top of burger. Spread glue on tab surface facing you. Center and place bun on top of burger crust side up. Allow to dry. Flip over burger to top bun side. Erase all pencil lines. Glue sesame seeds to top bun if you wish, using paper punch to make them. Unfolded card should resemble drawing below.

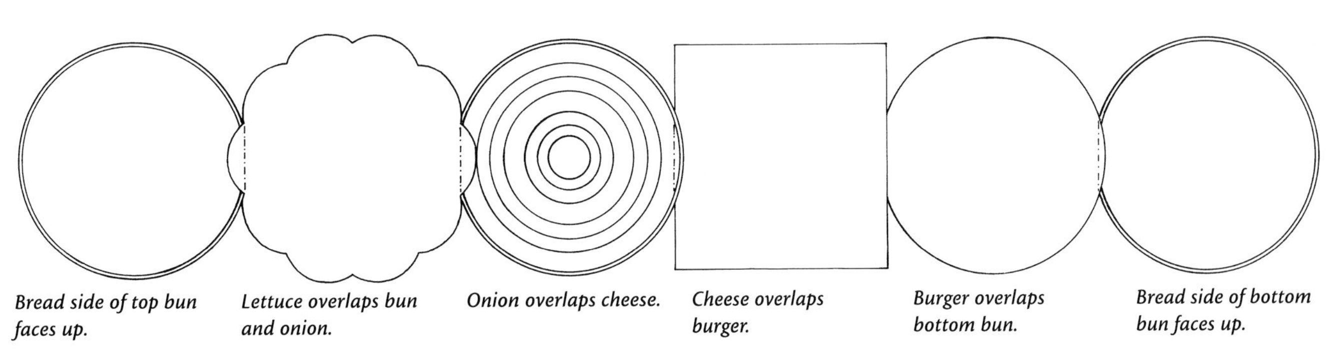

Unfolded Hamburger Note Card

Star Note Card or Place Card

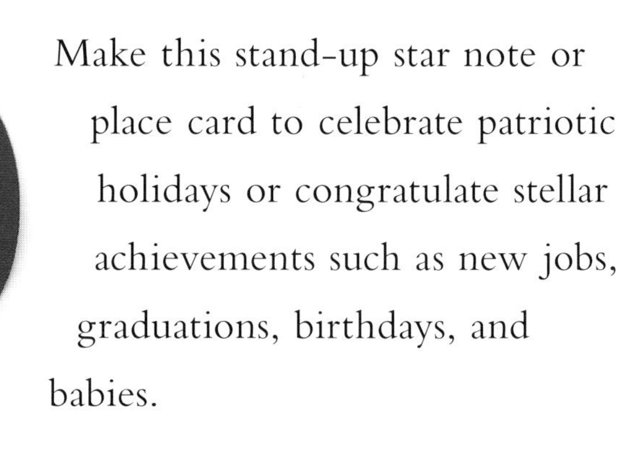

Make this stand-up star note or place card to celebrate patriotic holidays or congratulate stellar achievements such as new jobs, graduations, birthdays, and babies.

Instructions

1. Photocopy or trace star pattern, and cut out.
2. Referring to Drawing 1, make very light pencil line across center of paper. Tape or clip star on paper, aligning X-marked pattern edges with pencil line on paper, as in Drawing 2. Top of star will extend above line. Draw around shape and remove pattern. Carefully erase portion of pencil line that passes through star top.
3. Cut star using craft knife on protected work surface. Referring again to Drawing 2, very carefully cut only top rounded point of star above pencil line. Cut precisely on star outline in this top area, because over-cutting errors will show when card is finished and opened. Use craft knife to lightly score across paper, running knife along "score and fold" edges of star but lifting it at center so it doesn't run across top point of star.
4. Referring to Drawing 3, fold paper on folding lines. Clip or tape layers together so they won't shift. Cut out star on remaining drawing lines.

Materials

For one 4⅜″ (11.1 cm) note or one 2¾″ (6.9 cm) place card

Patterns on page 100

Equipment in work box, pages 4–6

3¼″ × 4″ (8.2 cm × 10.2 cm) piece of sturdy paper for place card

5″ × 6″ (12.7 cm × 15.2 cm) piece of sturdy paper for note

Envelope, 4¼″ × 5⅛″ (10.8 cm × 13.0 cm), or Envelope C pattern, page 83, and instructions, pages 80–83

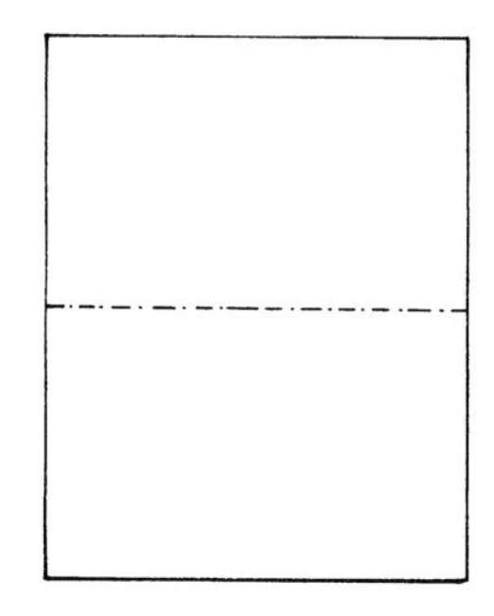

1. Mark pencil line midway across paper.

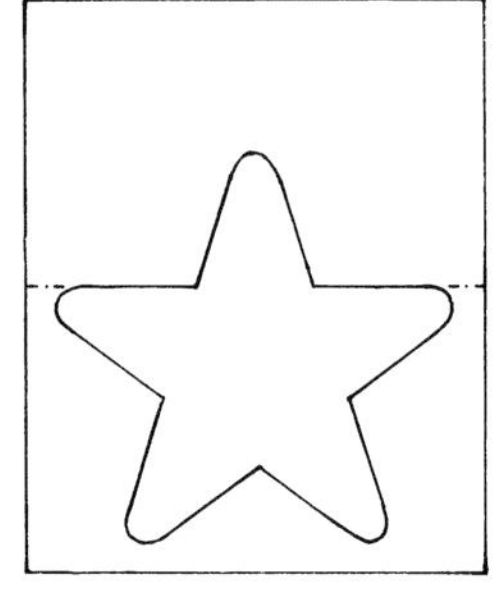

2. Place pattern on pencil line, draw star, and cut top point.

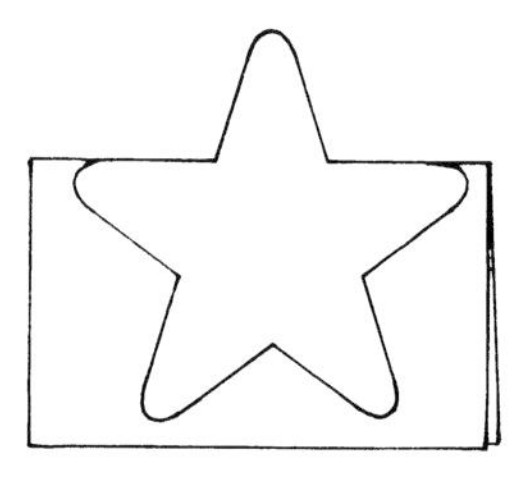

3. Fold paper and cut remaining points of star.

4

Autumn Notes

Etc Note

This folded note says it all! Duplex paper is cut and folded to make the letters stand out from the background like type on a printed page.

Materials

For one 6⅜″ × 11¾″ (16.2 cm × 29.8 cm) note

Pattern on page 101

Equipment in work box, pages 4–6

6½″ × 10½″ (16.5 cm × 26.7 cm) piece of duplex paper

Envelope, 3⅝″ × 6½″ (9.2 cm × 16.5 cm), or Envelope D pattern, page 83, and instructions, pages 80–83

Instructions

1. Photocopy or trace pattern and cut out.
2. Referring to Drawing 1, measure, mark, and score paper as indicated.
3. Referring to Drawing 2, fold paper as shown.
4. Unfold paper and place lettering color facing up. Tape or clip pattern on top area and trace around shape as in Drawing 3.
5. Remove pattern and place work on protected work surface. Use craft knife to cut out letters as in Drawing 4. Refold.

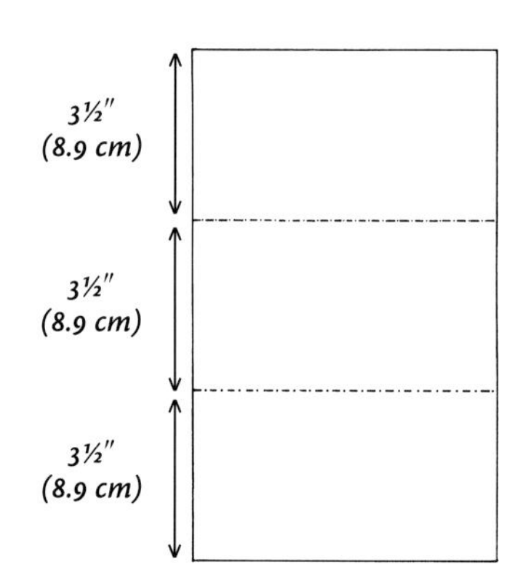

1. Measure, mark, and score paper.

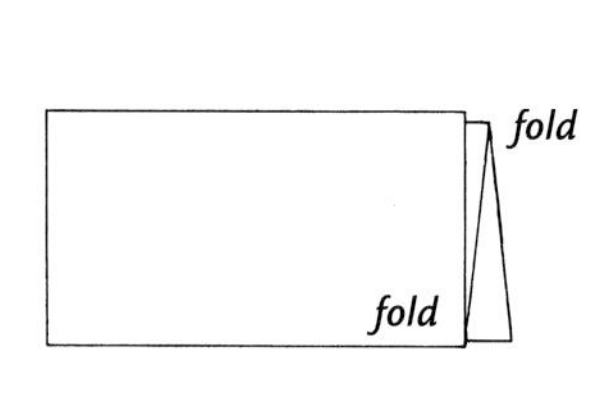

2. Fold paper.

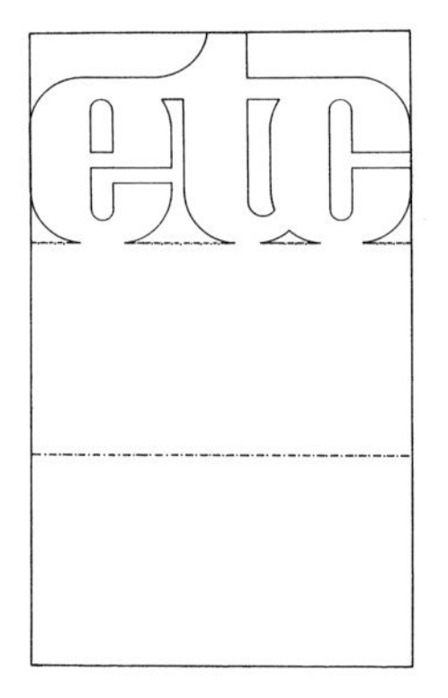

3. Draw around pattern.

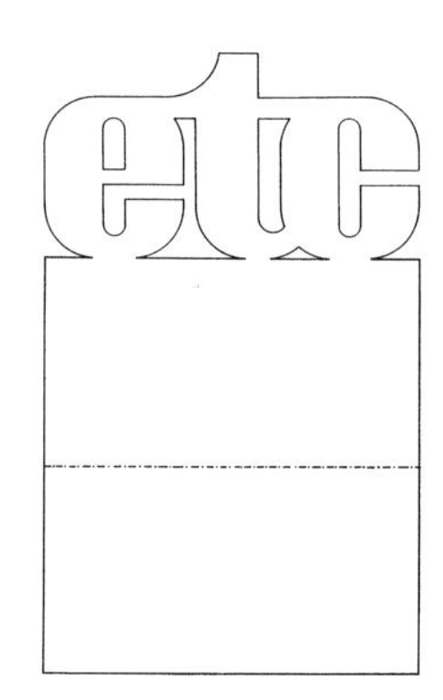

4. Cut around letters.

Pencil Note

Scribble a few quick words to a friend on this chubby pencil note. The pencil is an especially appropriate symbol for those of us who are somewhat technically challenged.

Materials

For one 2$\frac{13}{16}$″ × 6⅜″ (7.2 cm × 16.2 cm) pencil note

Patterns on page 101

Equipment in work box, pages 4–6

6¾″ (17.2 cm) square of tan paper, scored and folded in half

1¼″ × 3″ (3.2 cm × 7.7 cm) piece of foil paper

2½″ × 3″ (6.3 cm × 7.7 cm) piece of paper for pencil side

1½″ × 3″ (3.8 cm × 7.7 cm) piece of paper for eraser

3″ (7.7 cm) square of dark paper for tip and trim

Envelope, 3⅝″ × 6½″ (9.2 cm × 16.5 cm), or Envelope D pattern, page 83, and instructions, pages 80–83

Instructions

1. Referring to Drawing 1, trace master pattern for entire pencil shape. Referring to Drawing 2, trace individual patterns for eraser, side of pencil, band, and tip. If photocopying master pattern, make two copies so one pencil shape can be cut apart to make individual patterns for pencil parts.
2. Place master pattern for entire pencil shape on tan paper, aligning "place on fold" edge of pattern with folded edge of paper. Hold pattern in place with removable tape or paper clips. Draw around outside edge of pattern and remove it. Hold folded paper layers together with paper clips and cut out shape.
3. Using technique described in Step 2, trace and cut out one eraser, one pencil side, one foil band, and one tip. Glue pieces in place on card.
4. To make trim, cut two ¼″ × 3″ (0.6 cm × 7.7 cm) strips of dark paper and glue in place on foil band. Cut trimming strips flush with sides of card.
5. To suggest faceting on pencil side, fine lines can be embossed on paper. Do this work on reverse side of paper and firmly draw straight pencil lines with help of straight edge. First check process on scrap paper to be sure pencil color will not appear on front of paper. Dull table knife can be used in place of pencil.

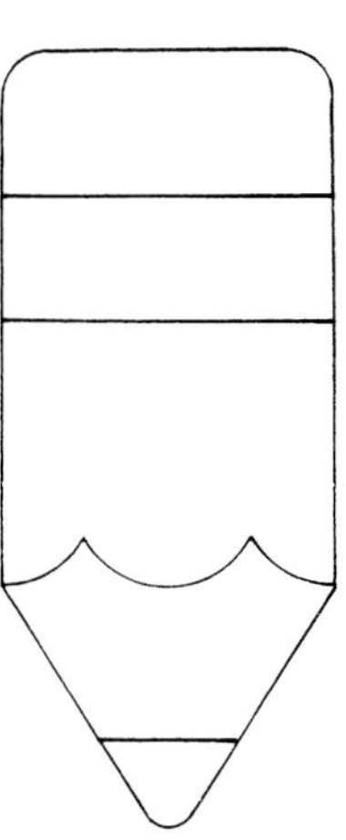

1. Trace master pattern.

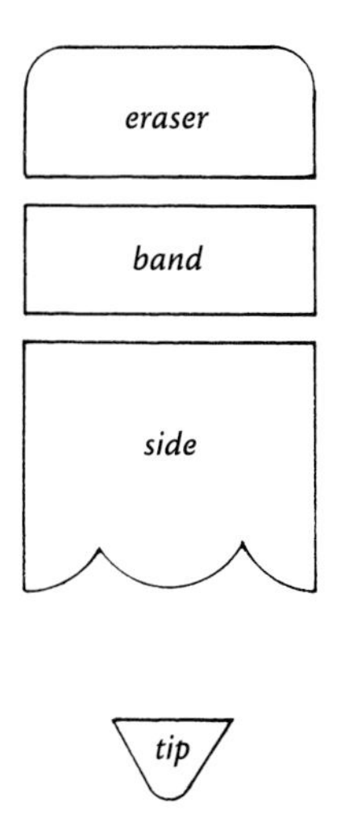

2. Trace individual patterns.

Materials

For one 3″ × 6⅛″ (7.7 cm × 15.5 cm) invitation

Patterns on page 102

Equipment in work box, pages 4–6

Two 3½″ × 6¾″ (8.9 cm × 17.1 cm) pieces of sturdy orange paper

Two 2″ × 3½″ (5.1 cm × 8.9 cm) pieces of lightweight white paper

Two 2″ × 3½″ (5.1 cm × 8.9 cm) pieces of lightweight yellow paper

Envelope, 3⅝″ × 6½″ (9.2 cm × 16.5 cm), or Envelope D pattern, page 83, and instructions, pages 80–83

Candy Corn Projects

Who can resist nibbling sweet little kernels of candy corn when Halloween is near? The distinct color and shape of this classic treat also make it an irresistible design motif for seasonal cards and decorations. Use a single kernel to make a party invitation or create a candy corn star ornament by clustering five kernels together.

Candy Corn Invitation

Instructions

1. Trace or photocopy pattern and glue to acetate if you wish. Cut out pattern to make card front.
2. To make card front, place one piece of orange paper on work surface, reserving second piece for card back. Glue white paper at top of orange paper, aligning top and side edges of both papers. Glue yellow paper at bottom of same piece of orange paper, aligning bottom and side edges of both papers. Tape or clip pattern on multicolored paper unit, aligning dotted placement lines on pattern with

color blocks on glued paper unit. Trace around outside edge of pattern and set unit aside.

3. To make card back, repeat step 2, using reserved pieces of paper. On reverse side of unit, draw pencil line across top of paper 2″ (5.1 cm) down from top 3½″ (8.9 cm) edge. Score and fold paper on pencil line.
4. Spread glue above folding line on reverse side of card back. Press reverse side of card front in place on glue area of card back, aligning all edges, and allow to dry. Use paper clips to hold card front and back layers together. Cut out candy corn shape.
5. To make cat liner for envelope, trace or photocopy pattern on folded paper and cut out. Score and fold 6″ (15.2 cm) square of purple paper in half and unfold. Place unfolded pattern on unfolded paper. Align horizontal folding line under eyes on pattern with folding line on paper. Draw around shape and within eyes. Cut out cat and inside eyes. Glue cat in place inside envelope, aligning folding lines and referring to instructions on pattern. Use paper punch to make stars for eyes.

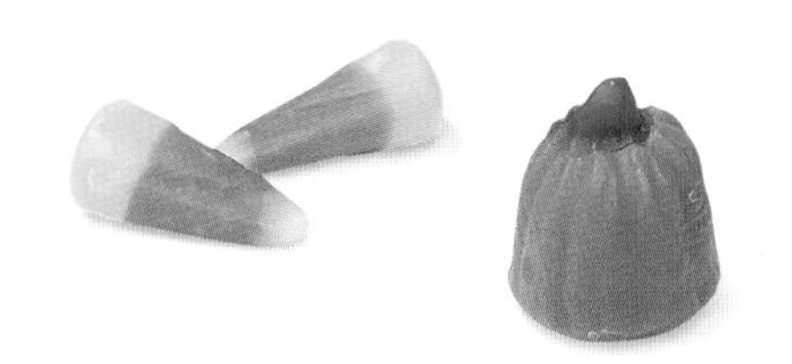

Candy Corn Star

Instructions

1. Trace or photocopy patterns and glue to acetate if you wish. Cut out both patterns.
2. On first square of yellow paper, measure and draw pencil line ¾″ (1.9 cm) from top edge. On second square of yellow paper, measure and draw pencil line ¾″ (1.9 cm) from top edge and then score and fold paper on pencil line. Unfold paper and spread glue on entire narrow area above folding line. Place first square on top of second, aligning all edges. Pencil line on top (first) paper should align with folding line on overlapped (second) paper.
3. Place star pattern on yellow square unit, aligning folding line indicated on pattern with folding line on paper. Anchor pattern on paper with tape or clips. Draw around star shape and remove pattern but not clips. Cut out unit starting at center opening. Flip star over to reverse (no-fold) side and set it aside.
4. Glue white paper strip on orange paper strip, aligning top edges. Place kernel pattern on white and orange striped unit so dotted placement line on pattern aligns with line where colors meet. Draw around edge of kernel. Remove pattern and cut out shape. Repeat to make total of five kernels. Glue one kernel in place on each point of reserved star. At star top, sandwich ends of hanging loop between star and kernel papers. Trim kernels to align with star edges if necessary.

Materials

For one 4⁹⁄₁₆″ (11.6 cm) diameter card or ornament

Patterns on page 102

Equipment in work box, pages 4-6

Two 4¾″ (12.0 cm) squares of yellow paper

¾″ × 5½″ (1.9 cm × 14.0 cm) piece of lightweight white paper

1¾″ × 5½″ (4.4 cm × 14.0 cm) piece of lightweight orange paper

6″ (15.2 cm) length of monofilament for hanging loop, optional

Envelope, 4¼″ × 5⅛″ (10.8 cm × 13.0 cm), or Envelope C pattern, page 83, and instructions, pages 80-83

Best Witches Card

Paper doll witches join hands to create a pint-sized Halloween parade. The simple silhouetted figures are very easy to cut. Then, separately cut brims are folded and slid over the witches' pointy hats. Patterns and instructions to make a pumpkin liner for the envelope are also included.

Materials

For one 2⅞″ × 5½″ (7.3 cm × 14.0 cm) folded card

Patterns on page 103

Equipment in work box, pages 4–6

8″ × 11½″ (20.4 cm × 29.2 cm) piece of black paper (sparkles are optional, but nice)

Envelope, 3⅝″ × 6½″ (9.2 cm × 16.5 cm), or Envelope D pattern, page 83, and instructions, pages 80–83

Instructions

1. Trace or photocopy patterns. Glue them to acetate if you wish. Cut out patterns. Use pin to pierce slot cutting line on brim and brim placement line on witch.
2. Cut 1½″ × 11½″ (3.8 cm × 29.2 cm) piece of paper from larger piece and reserve for hat brims. Fold remaining 6½″ × 11½″ (16.5 cm × 29.2 cm) piece of paper in half crosswise and unfold. Bring both 6½″ (16.5 cm) edges of paper to meet at center folding line. Unfold.

3. Referring to Drawing 1, accordion-fold paper on existing folding lines. Place witch pattern on paper with arms touching side edges as in Drawing 1 on page 53. Hold pattern in place with tape or paper clips. Draw around outside edge of pattern. Remove pattern but replace clips to hold paper layers together. Working on protected surface and making multiple passes with craft knife if necessary, cut out witch shape. Unfold card and flip it over to reverse side of paper. Use straightedge and craft knife to score folding line at top of each set of feet along bottom of each skirt, and then fold up feet against right side of each skirt. Hold pattern against reverse side of each witch and use pencil dots to transfer brim placement line on every head. Set piece aside.
4. Cut four hat brims from reserved piece of black paper, first tracing shape and then transferring slot cutting line with pencil dots placed in pinholes. Brims can be cut all at once if four 1½″ × 2½″ (3.8 cm × 6.4 cm) pieces of black paper are stacked and taped separately onto protected work surface. Cut slot in each brim from dot to dot. Score folding lines that extend beyond slot from edge to edge of brims. Fold brims with right side on outside and slide one over each pointy hat. Set unit aside.
5. From black paper scraps cut four ¼″ × ⅞″ (0.6 cm × 2.2 cm) pieces to use as brim hinges. Score folding line lengthwise through center of each strip and fold. Referring to Drawing 2 and working on reverse side of heads, glue hinge on each witch, overlapping both unfolded brim and head with hinge. Folding line of hinge should align with folding line of brim. Allow to dry.
6. Turn witches to right side. Unfold feet so they are at right angles to skirts. Lift brims so they are folded like little tents over faces. Stand witches on tabletop in zigzag array. When placing witches in envelope, fold down brims so faces are covered. Fold up feet and accordion-fold witches.
7. To make pumpkin liner for envelope, trace or photocopy pumpkin and stem patterns and cut out. Score and fold 6″ (15.2 cm) square of orange paper in half. Align "place on fold" edge of pattern with folded edge of paper. Draw around shape and within eyes. Clip paper layers together and cut out pumpkin but not eyes. Unfold paper and cut out eyes. Glue pumpkin in place inside envelope. Trace and cut out one stem from green paper scrap. Glue in place at pumpkin top.

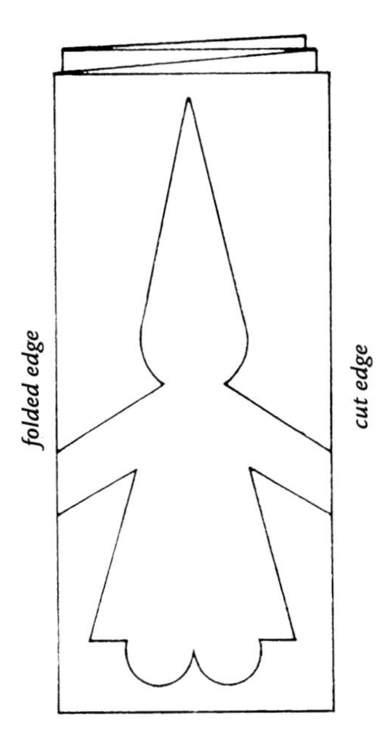

1. Accordion-fold paper and draw witch.

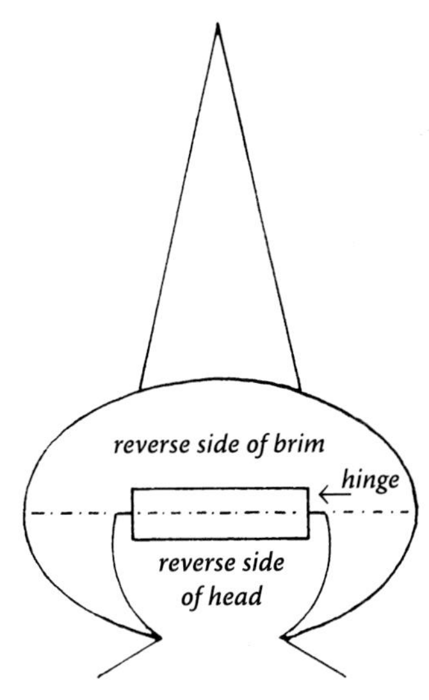

2. Glue hinge on reverse side of each head and brim.

Cat Card

This not-just-for-Halloween cat is made to stand up on its own. Using the pattern provided, you can make a cat wearing a pumpkin mask and then try the other two playful variations: a patched cat and one that looks like a painted pull-toy.

Materials

For one 3⅞″ × 4″ (9.8 cm × 10.2 cm) cat card

Patterns on page 104

Equipment in work box, pages 4–6

Two 5″ (12.7 cm) squares of sturdy paper for cat

2″ (5.1 cm) square of paper for mask, optional

White and black fine-line felt-tip pens

Crochet cotton or fine string

Paper punch, ⅛″ (0.3 cm) diameter

Star-shaped paper punch, ½″ (1.3 cm) diameter, for wheel centers, optional

Envelope, 4¼″ × 5⅛″ (10.8 cm × 13.0 cm), or Envelope C pattern, page 83, and instructions, pages 80–83

Instructions

1. Trace or photocopy patterns and glue them to acetate if you wish. Cut out patterns. Cut out face on pumpkin mask and eyes on cat. Pierce cat mouth and nose lines with pin.
2. On right side of first large square of paper, measure and draw pencil line 2½″ (6.4 cm) from top edge. Place second large square of paper right-side up on work surface. Measure and draw pencil line 2½″ (6.4 cm) from top edge and then score and fold paper on pencil line. Unfold paper and spread glue on entire area above folding line. Place first square on top of second square, aligning all edges. Pencil line on top (first) paper should align with folding line on overlapped (second) paper.
3. Place cat pattern on large square unit, aligning folding line indicated on pattern with pencil line on paper. Anchor pattern on paper with tape or clips. Draw around cat shape and transfer eyes, nose, and mouth if you wish. Remove pattern but not clips. Cut out cat and gently erase pencil line.
4. To make mask for cat, place mask pattern on 2″ (5.1 cm) paper scrap, and draw around shape and within facial features. Cut out pumpkin face and glue contrasting paper behind it if you wish. Cut out mask and pierce holes on sides. Cut skinny strip of paper to use as mask string. Glue piece of "string" within hole on each side edge of mask. Glue mask on face and glue ends of "string" on reverse side of cat head.

5. To make pull-toy cat, use instructions in step 4 to cut and apply mask, with real string if you wish. To make wheels for pull-toy, cut four ⅞″ (2.2 cm) diameter circles of paper and glue one in place on each foot. Use ½″ (1.3 cm) paper punch to cut stars for wheel centers and glue them in place. Use ⅛″ (0.3 cm) diameter paper punch to make four dots and glue them to centers of stars. Cut length of string and glue one end between paper layers at cat neck. At other end of string, encase cut end within two punched-out paper dots or stars.
6. To make patched cat, use fine-line white felt-tip pen to draw nose, mouth, and stitches around cat shape. Use ⅛″ (0.3 cm) diameter circle paper punch to cut two button eyes and glue in place. Draw holes in buttons with black fine-line pen. Use decorative paper punches to cut star patches and glue on cat. Draw stitches around patches with white fine-line pen.

Apron Note Cards

Pleasant memories of home are symbolized with these homespun apron notes, making them perfect for nostalgic occasions such as Thanksgiving and other family celebrations.

Materials

For one 4¼″ × 5¼″ (10.8 cm × 13.3 cm) note card

Patterns on page 104

Equipment in work box, pages 4-6

4½″ × 11″ (11.4 cm × 27.9 cm) piece of sturdy paper for apron

4¼″ × 5¼″ (10.8 cm × 13.3 cm) piece of patterned paper for overlay, if desired

Scrap paper for utensils

20″ (50.9 cm) length of ¼″ (0.6 cm) wide twill tape or ribbon

Envelope, 4⅜″ × 5¾″ (11.1 cm × 14.6 cm), or Envelope B pattern, page 82, and instructions, pages 80-82

Instructions

1. To make kitchen note, trace pattern for apron card. Make second, somewhat smaller overlay pattern by tracing dotted apron shape just inside card outline. Also trace patterns for small pocket, pocket overlay, and utensils.
2. Score and fold solid color paper in half crosswise. Align "place on fold" edge of apron pattern on folded edge of paper. Use removable tape to anchor pattern on paper, and draw around shape with pencil. Remove pattern. Hold folded paper layers together with tape or paper clips. Cut out apron. On inside of card score folding line only across apron back. Apron front should not fold. Cut one pocket from scrap of apron paper. Set apron and pocket aside.
3. Use same method on single layer of patterned paper to trace and cut out one apron overlay and one pocket overlay. Center these overlays on apron and pocket pieces and glue in place. Spread thin line of glue on lower and side edges of pocket and place on apron.
4. Cut twill tape or ribbon into one 5½″ (14.0 cm) piece and two 7¼″ (18.4 cm) pieces. Cut small slots on folding line at apron top as indicated on pattern. Slide ¼″ (0.6 cm) of cut ends of smallest piece of twill tape into each slot and glue in place on apron front, inside card. Glue one cut end of each of remaining tapes inside card on apron front at waist. Spread glue on entire area above folding line inside card on apron back. Hold front and back together until dry. Ties will be sandwiched between layers.
5. Cut utensils from scrap paper and insert in apron pocket.
6. To make garden apron, omit overlay paper and cut long large pocket instead of small one. Spread thin line of glue on bottom and side edges of pocket and place on lower edge of apron. Draw tiny stitches around edges using opaque white pen. Insert folded seed pack or trowel cut from paper scrap into pocket.

Standing House Card

This simple two-piece construction folds flat for mailing yet will stand up as a three-dimensional house when taken from the envelope and coaxed into shape. Use this card for a haunted house invitation, an open house announcement, or a welcome home greeting for a friend. Leave the window cutouts as they are or back them with pretty paper, a lace paper doily, or a glow-in-the-dark paper scrap.

Instructions

1. Trace or photocopy patterns and glue them to acetate if you wish. Cut out patterns. Cut out windows on house and chimney slot on roof. Use pin to make small holes marking glue tab placement area on roof and folding lines on both patterns.
2. Tape or clip house pattern on house paper. Trace around pattern and within windows. Transfer placement of folding lines with pencil dots pushed into pattern pinholes. Remove pattern. Use craft knife on protected work surface to cut out house. Score horizontal folding line and all short vertical folding lines. Cut out windows. Flip over house to reverse side. Center and glue window backing paper in place if you wish. Hold reversed pattern against cutout shape, transfer long vertical folding lines from each peak to house base, and then score lines.
3. Fold scored lines on house. Place glue on side tab, form house, and hold until dry. Set house aside.
4. Place roof pattern on roof paper and draw shape, transferring placement of chimney slot and folding line. Remove pattern and cut out roof and chimney slot. Flip roof over to reverse side, hold pattern against it, and transfer glue tab placement area with pencil dots. Connect dots to draw glue tab area. Fold roof on scored line and then unfold it.
5. Place unfolded roof (chimney slot at top) right-side down on work surface. On reserved house, spread glue on right side of roof glue tab. Align and press glue tab on glue-tab placement area of roof. When dry, fold roof to front of house, sliding chimney slot over chimney.

Materials

For one standing 1¾″ × 3¼″ × 3¾″ (4.4 cm × 8.2 cm × 9.5 cm) house card

Patterns on pages 105–106

Equipment in work box, pages 4–6

4¼″ × 10¾″ (10.8 cm × 27.3 cm) piece of paper for house

4½″ × 5″ (11.4 cm × 12.7 cm) piece of paper for roof

1½″ × 2¾″ (3.8 cm × 6.9 cm) piece of paper for backing windows, optional

Envelope, 4¼″ × 5⅛″ (10.8 cm × 13.0 cm), or Envelope C pattern, page 83, and instructions, pages 80–83

Kitchen Note Cards

Thoughts of country kitchens and church suppers come to mind with this heaping bowl of mashed potatoes. The spoon is removable and the bowl is hinged so the card will stand upright. Three small kitchen utensils slide into a pocket at the top of the crock note. A favorite recipe can be folded and tucked in as well.

Materials

For one 3⅞″ × 4¼″ (9.8 cm × 10.8 cm) card

Patterns on page 106

Equipment in work box, pages 4–6

5″ (12.7 cm) square of sturdy paper for bowl

1″ × 5″ (2.5 cm × 12.7 cm) piece of paper for bowl trim lines, or felt-tip pen

5″ (12.7 cm) square of paper for potatoes

1½″ × 4½″ (3.8 cm × 11.4 cm) piece of sturdy paper for spoon

Paper punch, ⅛″ (0.3 cm) diameter

Envelope, 4¼″ × 5⅛″ (10.8 cm × 13.0 cm), or Envelope C pattern, page 83, and instructions, pages 80–83

Mashed Potatoes Card

Instructions

1. Trace or photocopy patterns for bowl, potatoes, and spoon, transferring all markings. Use pin to pierce trim lines on bowl at intervals. Pierce placement lines for bowl rim and curved slot on potatoes.
2. Score and fold in half papers for bowl and potatoes. For both bowl and potatoes, align "place on fold" edge of patterns with folded edge of papers. Use removable tape to anchor patterns on papers, and draw around shapes with pencil. Push pencil into pinholes to transfer placement lines. On bowl, mark two dots on top folded edge to indicate slot cutting line. Remove patterns. Lightly draw all placement lines by connecting dots. Use craft knife on protected work surface to cut out bowl and potatoes. Cut out one spoon. Also cut out six 1⁄16″ × 5″ (0.2 cm × 12.7 cm) strips for bowl trim lines, if desired. Alternatively, stripes can be added with felt-tip pen.
3. Unfold bowl so right side of front and back faces you. Cut slot along top folding line from dot to dot, leaving ¼″ (0.6 cm) uncut margins at each end of slot. Refold bowl and set aside. Unfold potatoes and cut small, curved slot on one surface only. This will be card front. Refold potatoes. On front only of folded potatoes, spread glue on entire area below straight placement line. Slide potatoes into slot at bowl top, aligning

placement line on potatoes with bowl top rim. Press firmly and allow to dry. Inside card, potatoes should be glued only to card front. Refold card and flip it over to card back. Use one long strip of transparent tape to close opening of bowl rim, joining it to potatoes.

4. On card front glue trim lines in place or draw stripes with felt-tip pen. Insert spoon in potatoes.

Crock Note

Materials

For one 2⅝″ × 6″ (6.7 cm × 15.2 cm) note

Patterns on page 107

Equipment in work box, pages 4–6

3″ × 9½″ (7.7 cm × 24.1 cm) piece of sturdy paper for crock

½″ × 2¾″ (1.3 cm × 6.9 cm) piece of paper for stripe trim

Felt-tip pen for trimming utensils, optional

Three 1½″ × 6¼″ (3.8 cm × 15.9 cm) pieces of sturdy paper for utensils

Envelope, 3⅝″ × 6½″ (9.2 cm × 16.5 cm), or Envelope D pattern, page 83, and instructions, pages 80–83

Instructions

1. Photocopy or trace patterns and cut out. Use pin to pierce rim line and stripe-trim placement lines in a few places.
2. Referring to Drawing 1, score crock paper at 3⅛″ (8.0 cm) intervals and label resulting panels A, B, and C. Referring to Drawing 2, accordion-fold paper as shown.
3. Align crock pattern on paper, holding it in place with paper clips or removable tape. Draw around shape, transferring lines with pencil placed in pinholes. Remove pattern.
4. Anchor folded card layers together with tape or clips. Use craft knife on protected work surface to cut out crock shape. To form pocket at crock top, place line of glue along crock side edges between panels A and B. Hold in place until dry.
5. Use blunt table knife or dull edge of ruler to "draw" indentation along rim line of crock. Test this process first on scrap paper. Glue stripe-trim line in place. When dry, trim ends of stripe flush with edges of crock.
6. Tape or clip utensil patterns to paper. Draw around shapes, remove patterns, and cut out.

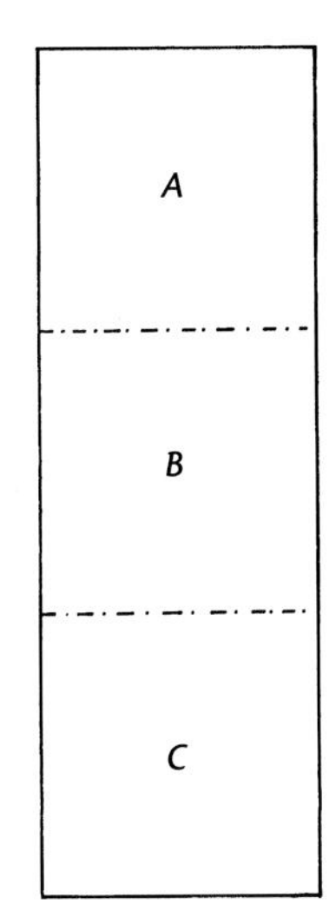

1. Measure and score panels on card.

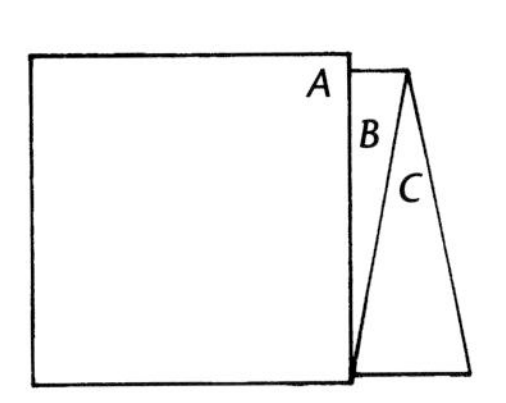

2. Accordion-fold card.

Scrap Paper Quilt Note Cards

Save even the smallest scraps of beautiful papers and then patch them together to make these log cabin quilt block note cards. These examples are made with little bits of Japanese chiyogami paper. Because the squares overlap, scrap pieces of paper with imperfect edges and missing corners can be used.

Materials

For one 4¼″ (10.8 cm) square note

Equipment in work box, pages 4-6

4¼″ × 8½″ (10.8 cm × 21.6 cm) piece of sturdy paper for card

Square scraps of lightweight paper:
2½″ (6.4 cm)
2″ (5.1 cm)
1½″ (3.8 cm)
1″ (2.5 cm)
½″ (1.2 cm)

Envelope, 4⅜″ × 5¾″ (11.1 cm × 14.6 cm), or Envelope B pattern, page 82, and instructions, pages 80-82

Note: See page 9 for chiyogami paper source.

Instructions

1. There is no pattern for this project. Score and fold sturdy paper in half crosswise to make 4¼″ (10.8 cm) square card. Use light pencil lines to draw 2½″ (6.4 cm) square at center of card front. Put card aside.
2. Starting with largest square and referring to Drawings 1 through 5, glue squares on top of squares. Center and glue largest square on card front. If patches do not visually separate enough from each other or from background, carefully outline patches with very fine, dark pencil lines.

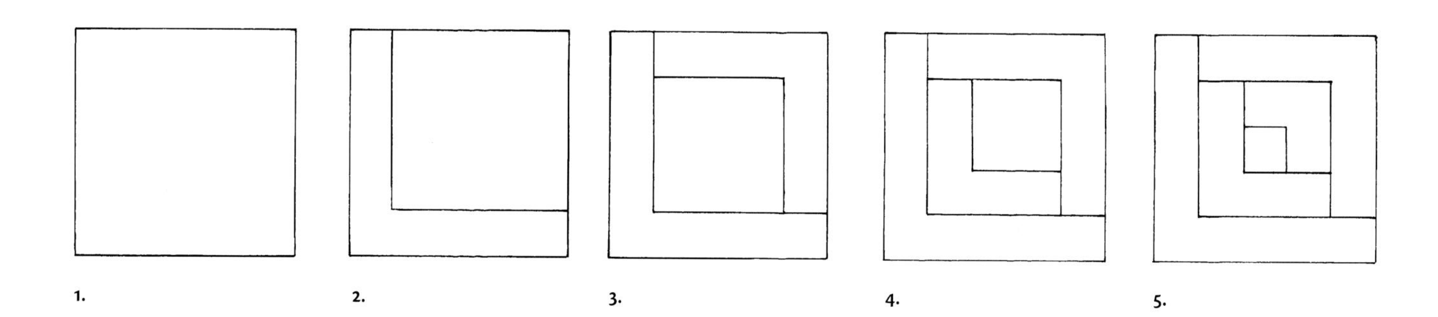

Get Well Teddy Card

This sick teddy with his fuzzy blanket and hot water bottle is sure to bring a smile to the face of a child in need of cheer. The hot water bottle, which opens like a little card, can be taken from teddy's paw to warm his tummy, and the velour blanket can be unfolded to make a cozy cover for him.

Materials

For one 3½″ × 5⅞″ (8.9 cm × 14.9 cm) card

Patterns on page 107

Equipment in work box, pages 4–6

6″ (15.2 cm) square of sturdy paper for teddy

Black fine-line felt-tip pen, optional

3¼″ × 4″ (8.2 cm × 10.2 cm) piece of paper for hot water bottle

4¼″ (10.8 cm) square of velour paper for blanket

3¾″ (9.5 cm) square of paper for overlay, optional

Envelope, 3⅝″ × 6½″ (9.2 cm × 16.5 cm), or Envelope D pattern, page 83, and instructions, pages 80–83

Instructions

1. Trace or photocopy patterns with markings and cut out. Mark arm line by piercing pattern with pin. Cut into paw lines and cut out eye.
2. Score and fold card paper in half with right side on outside. Align "place on fold" edge of teddy pattern with folded edge of card.
3. Cut out teddy. Cut arms and paws on solid pattern lines. Cut out eye and paw lines or use felt-tip pen to draw them.
4. To make hot water bottle, score and fold paper in half crosswise with right side on outside. Align "place on fold" edge of pattern with folded edge of paper. Trace around shape and cut out. Use dull table knife to emphasize straight horizontal lines at top, neck, and bottom of hot water bottle if you wish. Message can be written inside hot water bottle before tucking it under teddy's arm.
5. Score and fold velour paper in quarters with right side on outside. If adding overlay, also score and fold overlay paper in quarters with print side facing up. Center and glue overlay on blanket. Fold blanket and tuck under teddy's arm. Use removable tape inside card to hold blanket and hot water bottle in place for mailing.

5

Winter Cheer

Snow Crystal Card

The true name of this 1870s Feathered Star quilt pattern is Radiant Star, but even though there are eight points on the pattern instead of six, the design has always made me think of snow crystals. This project requires complete concentration as well as great accuracy.

Materials

For one 4¼″ (10.8 cm) folded card

Three photocopies of pattern on page 108

Equipment in work box, pages 4–6

4¼″ × 17″ (10.8 cm × 43.8 cm) piece of lightweight duplex paper

Envelope, 4⅜″ × 5¾″ (11.1 cm × 14.6 cm), or Envelope B pattern, page 82, and instructions, pages 80–82

Note: If you are unable to locate 4¼″ × 17″ (10.8 cm × 43.8 cm) duplex paper, use an 8½″ × 11″ (21.6 cm × 27.9 cm) piece in its place. Cut as follows: one 4¼″ × 8½″ (10.8 cm × 21.6 cm) piece and one 4¼″ × 8¾″ (10.8 cm × 22.3 cm) piece. On one 4¼″ (10.8 cm) edge of larger piece, draw pencil line ¼″ (0.6 cm) from edge. Align one 4¼″ (10.8 cm) edge of smaller piece on pencil line of larger piece and glue papers together.

Instructions

1. To make card pattern, precisely cut out 4¼″ (10.8 cm) pattern square from each of three photocopies. Label one panel A, one panel B, and one panel C. Cut one additional 4¼″ (10.8 cm) piece of scrap paper for unmarked panel D pattern. Referring to Drawing 1, tape panels together side by side, in ABCD order.
2. Referring to Drawing 2, use pencil or marker to add color to outlined portion of snowflakes.
3. Referring to Drawing 3, accordion-fold pattern into card format. Hold folded pattern against lighted window to check alignment of edges and design motif on each panel. If card edges or design motifs don't align, make adjustments.
4. Tape duplex paper to work surface so inside surface of card faces up. With panel A on left, tape pattern in place on top of duplex paper. Cutting directly through pattern and duplex paper, cut out design motifs on panels A, B, and C as shown in Drawing 2. Use tiny pinholes to mark folding lines between each panel. Remove pattern. Score folding lines on duplex paper. Remove tape and accordion-fold card.

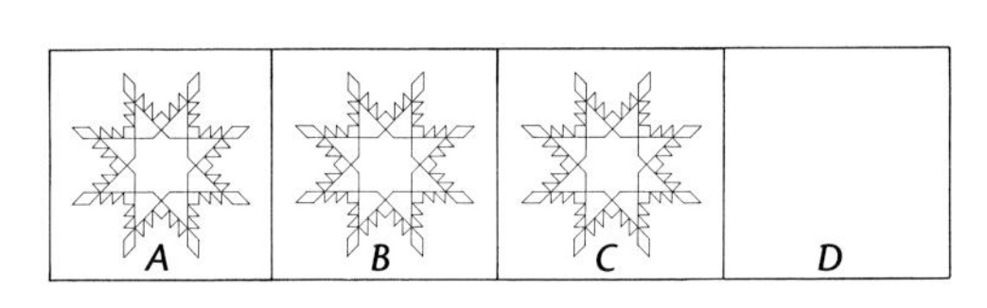

1. Tape photocopies together to make complete pattern. Inside of card faces up.

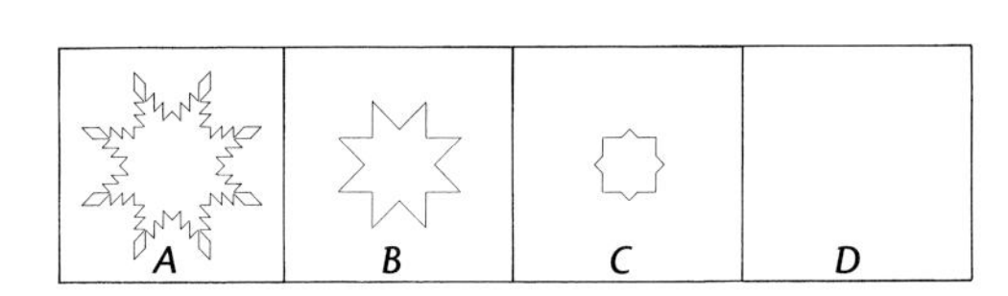

2. Add color to outlined shape on each panel to indicate cutting area.

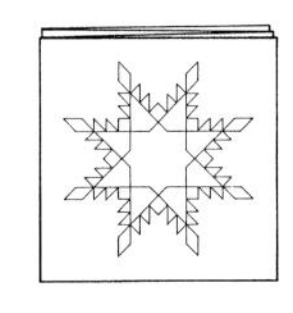

3. Accordion-fold pattern.

Sled Card

Coast down the snowy hills of memory lane with this miniature sled card. The top lifts up, providing a space for your greeting, and the runners fold flat underneath the card, making it easy to tuck the sled into an envelope and send it on its way.

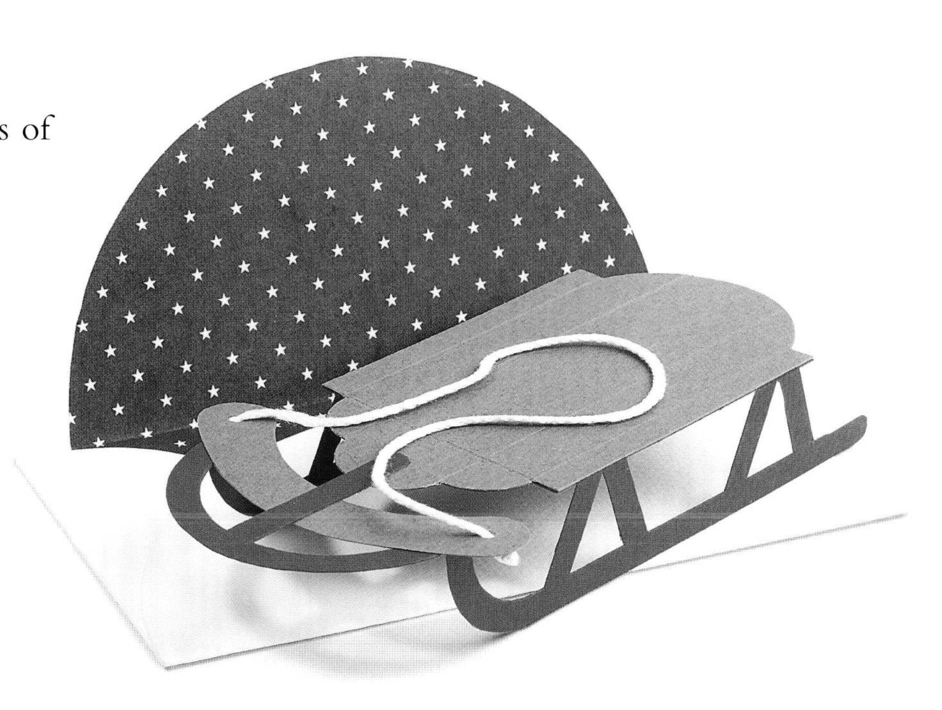

Instructions

1. Trace or photocopy patterns for sled top and runners, transferring all markings. Glue them to acetate. Pierce patterns with pin to indicate folding lines and outline of straight center bar with rounded end.
2. Use removable tape to anchor patterns on paper and use pencil to draw around shapes and inside runners. Push pencil into pinholes. Remove patterns. Finish drawing all lines indicated with pencil dots.
3. Cut out sled top and runner pieces with craft knife on protected work surface. On sled runner piece cut straight center tab (with rounded end) away from platform of runner. Cut out negative areas within sled runner piece and score and crease folding lines.
4. Score folding line on reverse side of sled top. Spread thin layer of glue on reverse side of sled top above folding line, and place it on platform area of flattened runner piece, aligning all edges. Lift straight center tab of runner piece up and over sled handlebars and glue it to sled top. Place dot of glue under each end of handlebar in order to glue handlebar ends to runners.
5. If you wish to indent board lines on sled top, use pin to pierce dotted lines on sled top pattern. Hold pattern against sled top and transfer dots by placing pencil in pattern holes. Remove pattern. Use straightedge and dull blade of kitchen knife to connect dots and indent lines. Also indent folding line.

Materials

For one 3¼″ × 6⅜″ (8.2 cm × 16.2 cm) sled card

Patterns on page 109

Equipment in work box, pages 4-6

3¾″ × 6″ (9.5 cm × 15.2 cm) piece of sturdy paper for sled top

5″ × 6¾″ (12.7 cm × 17.1 cm) piece of sturdy paper for sled runners

12″ (30.5 cm) length of thin cord

Envelope, 3⅝″ × 6½″ (9.2 cm × 16.5 cm), or Envelope D pattern, page 83, and instructions, pages 80-83

Note: To make sled very quickly, photocopy patterns and tape rough-cut patterns to paper. Cut out sled pieces directly through patterns.

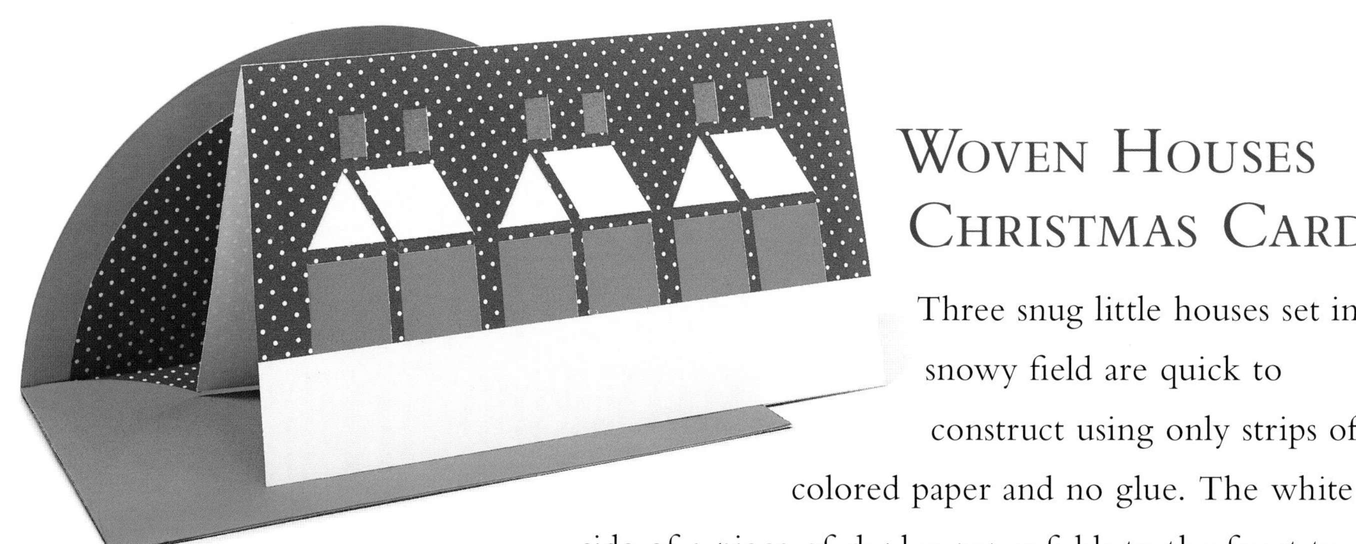

Woven Houses Christmas Card

Three snug little houses set in a snowy field are quick to construct using only strips of colored paper and no glue. The white side of a piece of duplex paper folds to the front to make the snowy field, and colorful strips of woven paper create a pattern of their own inside the card.

Materials

For one 3½″ × 6⅜″ (8.9 cm × 16.2 cm) card

Pattern on page 110

Equipment in work box, pages 4–6

6⅜″ × 8″ (16.2 cm × 20.4 cm) piece of duplex paper for card

¾″ × 6⅜″ (1.9 cm × 16.2 cm) piece of lightweight paper for houses

⅝″ × 6⅜″ (1.6 cm × 16.2 cm) piece of lightweight paper for roofs

⅜″ × 6⅜″ (1.0 cm × 16.2 cm) piece of lightweight paper for chimneys

Envelope, 3⅝″ × 6½″ (9.2 cm × 16.5 cm), or Envelope D pattern, page 83, and instructions, pages 80–83

Instructions

1. Trace or photocopy pattern, cut out, and set aside.
2. Referring to Drawing 1, draw folding lines on right side of paper.
3. Referring to Drawing 2, score and fold paper on folding line 1. Use tiny pin to pierce pattern at each end of folding line 2. Flip paper to reverse side and score and fold on folding line 2.
4. Unfold paper and place right side up on protected work surface as in Drawing 3. Tape or clip reserved pattern on card front area. Use craft knife and straight edge to cut slots through pattern.
5. On reverse side of card front, start with house color and weave paper strip through slots. Weave roof and chimney colored strips too. Fold card so narrow strip at bottom becomes snowy field on card front.

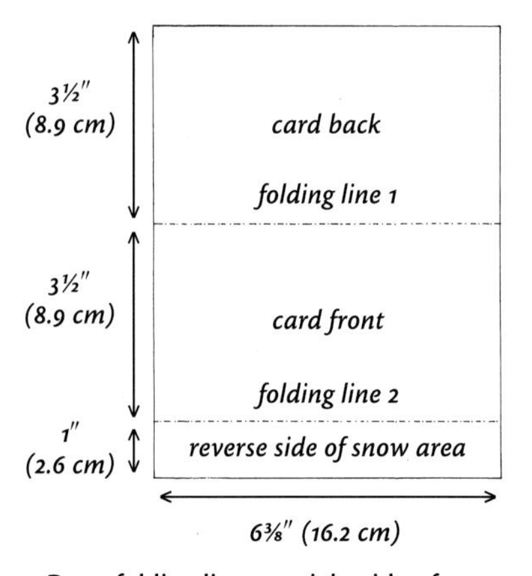

1. Draw folding lines on right side of paper.

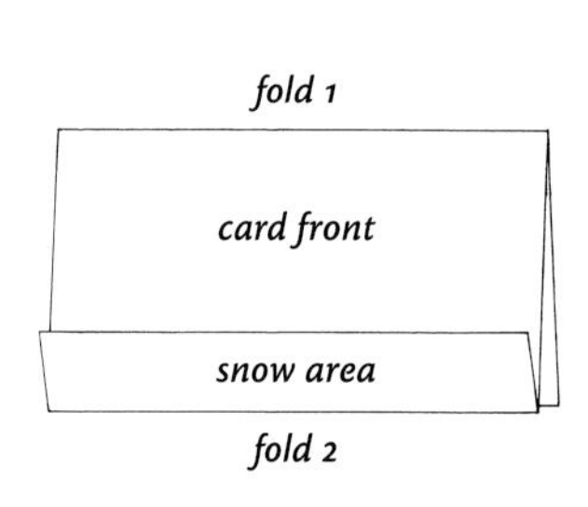

2. Score and fold paper.

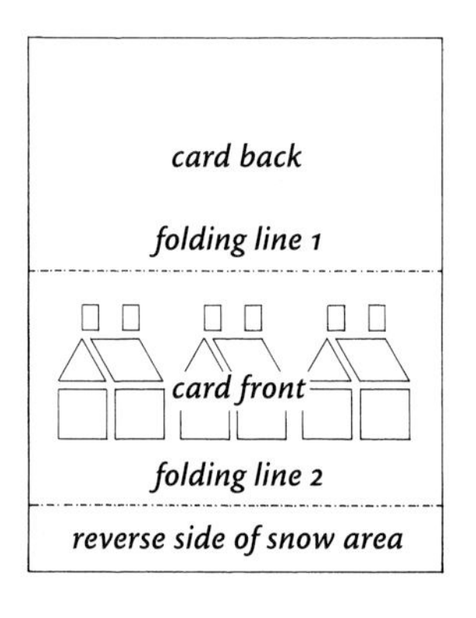

3. Unfold card and place pattern on front.

Christmas Cracker Card

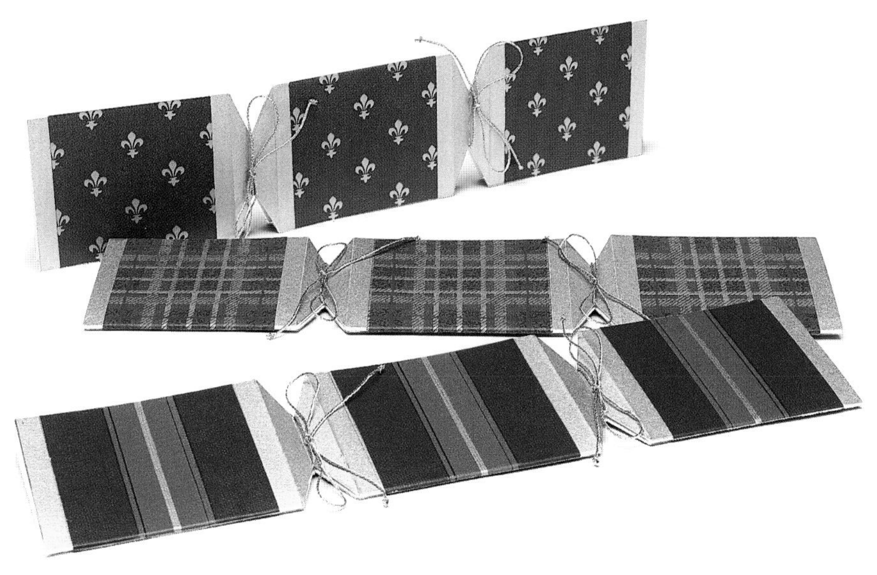

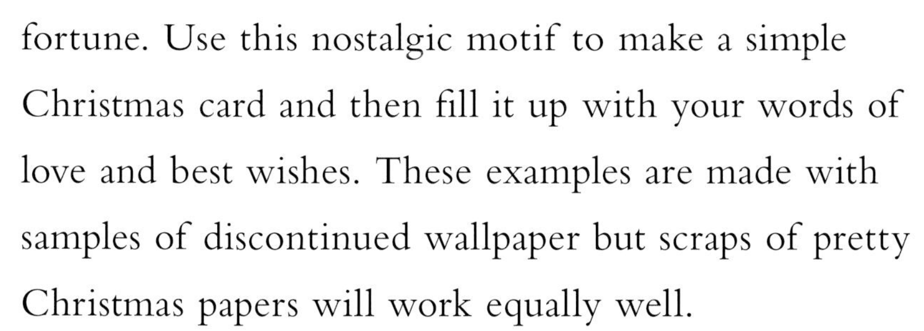

A tradition dating back to the mid-nineteenth century, Christmas crackers are usually filled with toys and treats as well as a paper hat and a poem or fortune. Use this nostalgic motif to make a simple Christmas card and then fill it up with your words of love and best wishes. These examples are made with samples of discontinued wallpaper but scraps of pretty Christmas papers will work equally well.

Materials

For one 2″ × 9¼″ (5.1 cm × 23.5 cm) card

Pattern on page 111

Equipment in work box, pages 4–6

4″ × 9¼″ (10.2 cm × 23.5 cm) piece of foil board, scored and folded in half lengthwise

Decorative paper scraps:
one piece 2¼″ × 4¼″ (5.7 cm × 10.8 cm)
two pieces 2⅛″ × 4¼″ (5.4 cm × 10.8 cm)

Two 13″ (33.0 cm) lengths of metallic cord or string

Envelope, 4⅛″ × 9½″ (10.5 cm × 24.1 cm)

Note: Unfold a store-bought envelope and use it as a pattern for creating your own unique envelope if you wish.

Instructions

1. On folded paper trace pattern with markings and cut out. Pierce folding lines and placement lines in several places with pin.
2. Tape or clip unfolded pattern on right side of unfolded foil board. Draw into V-areas. Using pencil point placed in pinholes, transfer folding lines A, B, and C as well as placement lines.
3. Remove pattern. Do not yet cut out V-areas. On foil side of unfolded card, score folding lines A and B. Also score folding line C, but use dull table knife instead of craft knife.
4. Flip card over to reverse (non-foil) side. Hold pattern against this surface and transfer folding lines A, B, and C. Use craft knife to score folding line C. Use dull table knife (not craft knife) to score folding lines A and B.
5. Flip card again to foil side. Fold card on A and B folding lines, making mountain folds. Fold card on C folding lines, making valley folds.
6. Flatten card and fold along top folding line. Tape or clip layers together and cut out V-areas.
7. Score and fold each piece of decorative paper in half crosswise. Use 2¼″ (5.7 cm) wide piece to overlap center section of cracker. Glue decorative paper in place, front and back. When dry, trim paper to align with bottom edge of card, front and back. Apply remaining papers in same way on end portions of cracker.
8. Tie cord around each end of cracker on folding line C. Knot ends of cord to prevent unraveling.

Christmas Ball Card

These Christmas ornament cards are very easy to make, and you can use all sorts of paper to create them: Japanese chiyogami paper, Italian marble paper, plain or embossed pieces of foil, and even snippets of wallpaper, gift wrap, and paper lace.

Materials

For one 3⅜″ × 4½″ (8.5 cm × 11.4 cm) card

Patterns on page 111

Equipment in work box, pages 4–6

4″ × 8½″ (10.2 cm × 21.6 cm) piece of sturdy paper (not cardboard)

3¾″ (9.5 cm) square of decorative paper

Paper punch, ¼″ (0.6 cm) diameter, for star-centered ornament

Envelope, 4¼″ × 5⅛″ (10.8 cm × 13.0 cm), or Envelope C pattern, page 83 and instructions, pages 80–83

Note: See page 9 for chiyogami paper source.

Instructions

1. Photocopy or trace patterns with markings and cut out. If making cut and folded star on ornament, use pin to pierce octagon shape on overlay pattern, making holes at each segment and at center of octagon. Also, use paper punch to cut holes in pattern.
2. Prepare sturdy paper by referring to Drawing 1. Place paper right-side up on protected work surface. Use pencil to draw folding line across midsection of paper leaving ½″ (1.3 cm) unmarked space at center. Score folding line, interrupting scoring at unmarked ½″ (1.3 cm) space. Do not fold paper.
3. Referring to Drawing 2, place ball base pattern on paper so straight top of ornament aligns with folding line and circular loop of ornament fits precisely within unscored space of folding line. Trace around pattern and remove it from paper.
4. Before folding paper, cut out and discard small circle within loop. Then cut outside edge of loop. Crease paper on folding line, allowing unfolded loop to rise above ornament as in Drawing 3. Tape or clip paper edges together and cut out ornament. Unfold card, flip it to reverse side, and reinforce top fold with clear tape. Add string or cord to loop if you wish.
5. Place ornament overlay pattern on reverse side of decorative paper, trace around shape and cut out. If making star cutout on overlay, go to step 6. If not making star, go to step 7.

6. If adding cut and folded star to overlay, transfer dots at center and segments of octagon by placing pencil point in pattern pinholes. Also transfer placement of punched out dots. Remove pattern and cut segments on solid lines. Lightly score folding lines (broken lines on pattern). Flip overlay to right side of paper. Fold back star segments so they rest on front of overlay. To make dot trim, first test paper punch on scrap of overlay paper. If punch does not cut well, use scrap of sturdy paper under overlay and punch dots from both layers at once. Reserve overlay paper dots; discard sturdy paper dots. Flip overlay paper dots to reverse (undecorative) side and glue in place as trim on star tips.
7. Glue overlay on card front. To make card stand up, trim along straight line on card back only. To define top of card front, use sharp pencil to outline scallops at top of overlay and to draw line at base of loop.

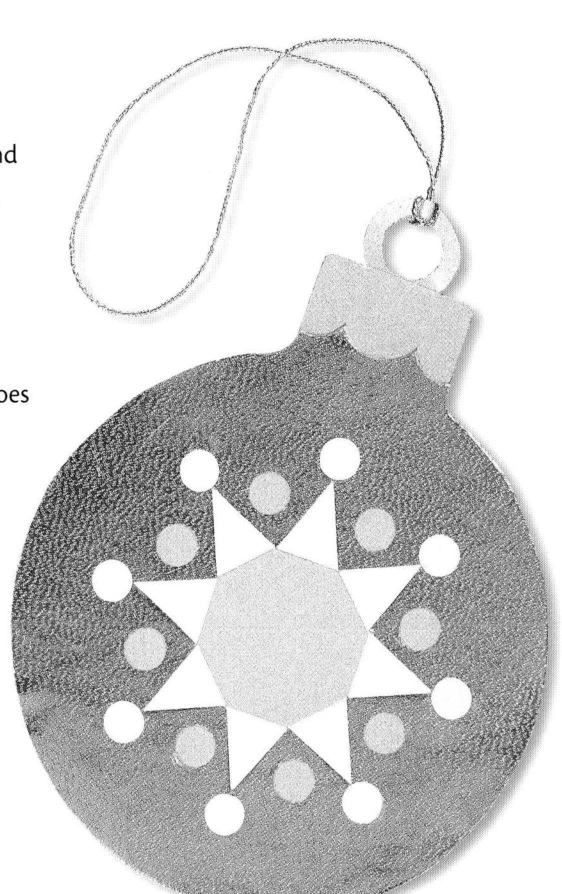

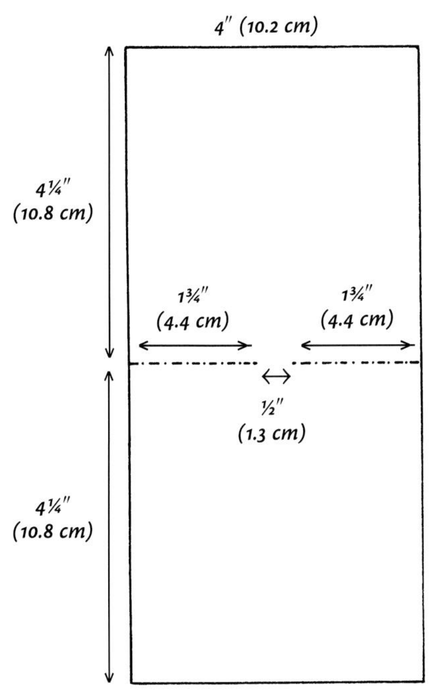

1. Score paper crosswise leaving ½" (1.3 cm) space unscored at center.

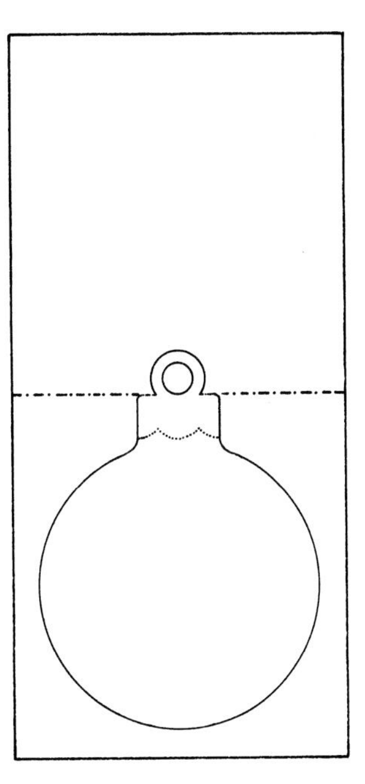

2. Draw ball base placing pattern as shown.

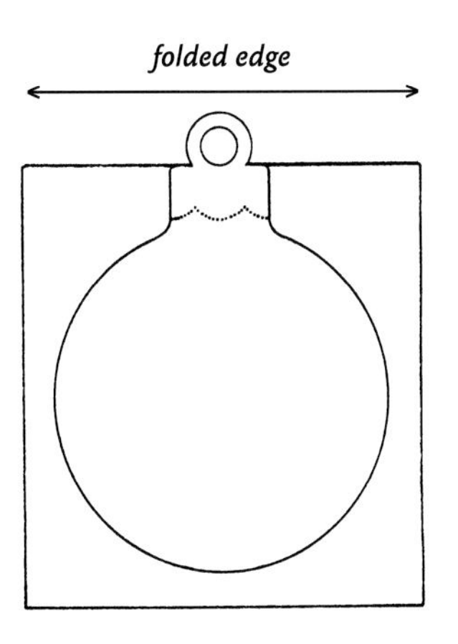

3. Cut out loop, fold paper, and cut out ornament.

Hanukkah Menorah Card

The menorah candles glow as bright symbols of faith on this Hanukkah greeting card. Make a few quick cuts and folds to create the stars, and then weave blue paper across the card's front to make the candles.

Materials

For one 3¼″ × 6 7⁄16″ (8.2 cm × 16.3 cm) card

Pattern on page 112

Equipment in work box, pages 4–6

6½″ × 6 7⁄16″ (16.5 cm × 16.3 cm) piece of sturdy, metallic duplex paper (not cardboard) for card

1¼″ × 7″ (3.2 cm × 17.8 cm) piece of blue paper for candles

Envelope, 3⅝″ × 6½″ (9.2 cm × 16.5 cm), or Envelope D pattern, page 83, and instructions, pages 80–83

Instructions

1. Trace or photocopy pattern and cut out.
2. On front surface of card, score and fold duplex paper in half crosswise to make 3¼″ × 6 7⁄16″ (8.2 cm × 16.3 cm) card with metallic surface inside.
3. Unfold card and tape it, metallic side up, to protected work surface. Tape pattern on card, aligning "place on fold" edge of pattern on folding line of card.
4. Using craft knife and straightedge and cutting right through pattern, cut eighteen vertical lines. Also cut pie-sliced units of intersecting lines at top of each candle. Remove pattern. Score folding lines at ends of pie slices, indicated with broken lines on pattern.
5. Flip paper over to front of card surface. Lift and fold back pie-sliced sections to create nine stars on card front.
6. Cut blue paper into one 1¼″ × 6½″ (3.2 cm × 16.5 cm) and one ⅜″ × ¾″ (1.0 cm × 1.9 cm) piece. Working on reverse side of card front, weave long strip of paper through slots. Weave short strip at top of center candle. Trim ends of strips to make them neat and aligned inside card.

Hanukkah Snowflake Card

A golden Star of David centered within a snowflake creates a simple Hanukkah greeting that can be made in two different ways. Cut out the snowflake motif, or cut out the hexagon shape leaving a border of golden triangles around the edge of the snowflake.

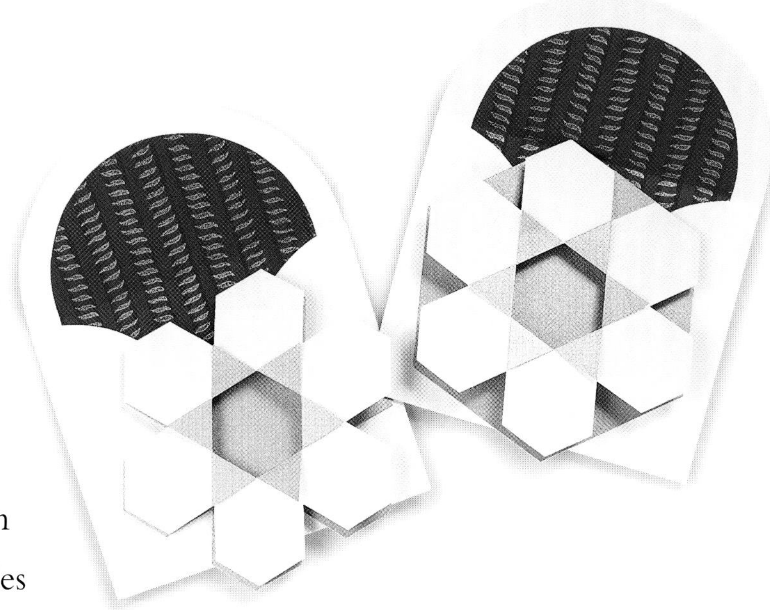

Materials

For one 4⅛″ × 4¾″ (10.5 cm × 12.0 cm) card

Pattern on page 112

Equipment in work box, pages 4–6

5½″ × 9″ (14.0 cm × 22.8 cm) piece of sturdy duplex paper (not cardboard)

Envelope, 4¼″ × 5⅛″ (10.8 cm × 13.0 cm), or Envelope C pattern, page 83, and instructions, pages 80–83

Instructions

1. Trace or photocopy pattern and rough cut around edges. Trim precisely on outline only along top "place on fold" edge of pattern.
2. Tape duplex paper vertically on protected work surface. Color for card front (not star color) should face up. Draw light pencil line across midsection of paper. Score pencil line with craft knife. Tape pattern onto duplex paper, aligning "place on fold" edge of pattern with scored line on paper.
3. If you wish to make snowflake-shaped card, go to step 4, omitting step 3. For hexagon-shaped card, using straightedge and craft knife and cutting right through pattern, cut pie-sliced intersecting lines at center of snowflake. Also cut out snowflake on unfolded card, but do not cut top edges of shape. Remove pattern. Flip card over to reverse side. Score folding lines at ends of pie slices, indicated with broken lines on patterns. Turn paper over to front surface again. Fold card on scored folding line at top of snowflake. Tape or clip paper layers together. Refer to photograph and use outer edges of snowflake as guide to cut out hexagon. Lift and fold back sliced sections to create star at center of card.
4. For snowflake-shaped card, using straightedge and craft knife and cutting right through pattern, cut pie-sliced intersecting lines at center of snowflake. Do not cut out snowflake. Leaving pattern in place, flip card paper over to reverse side. Score folding lines at end of pie slices, indicated with broken lines on pattern. Turn paper over to pattern side again. Fold card on scored line along top of pattern. Tape or clip paper layers together and cut out snowflake. Lift and fold back sliced selections to create star at center of card. To make faceted snowflake, score and fold from tip to tip on card front only.

Cathedral Window Christmas Cards

The edges of nine origami paper circles are folded to make nine square units for each variation of these Cathedral Window Christmas Cards. Make the 1¼″ (3.2 cm) circles with a compass or use a circle cutter for greater speed and accuracy.

Materials

For one 4¼″ (10.8 cm) square card

Equipment in work box, pages 4–6

4¼″ × 8½″ (10.8 cm × 21.6 cm) piece of sturdy white paper

Nine 1¼″ (3.2 cm) diameter circles cut from lightweight duplex or origami paper

Envelope, 4⅜″ × 5¾″ (11.1 cm × 14.6 cm), or Envelope B pattern, page 82, and instructions, pages 80–82

Note: There is no pattern for this project.

Instructions

1. Score and fold sturdy white paper in half crosswise to make 4¼″ (10.8 cm) square card. Use light pencil lines to draw 2⅝″ (6.7 cm) square at center of card front. Put card aside.
2. Referring to Drawings 1 through 8, fold circles into small squares and crease edges sharply. Glue small squares side by side within pencil lines at center of card front.

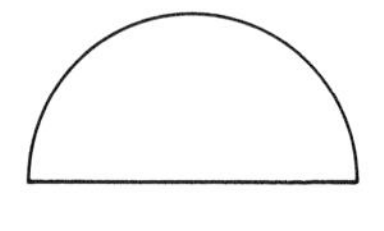

1. Fold circle in half.

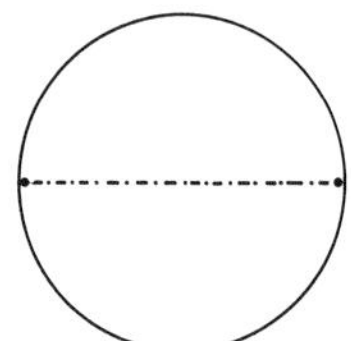

2. Unfold circle. Place dot precisely at each end of folding line on front and back of circle.

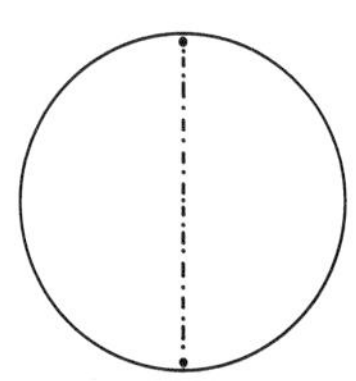

3. Rotate circle so folding line is in vertical position.

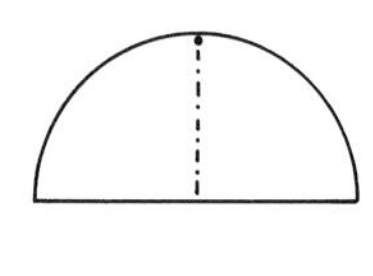

4. Fold circle in half again, aligning dots at end of first folding line.

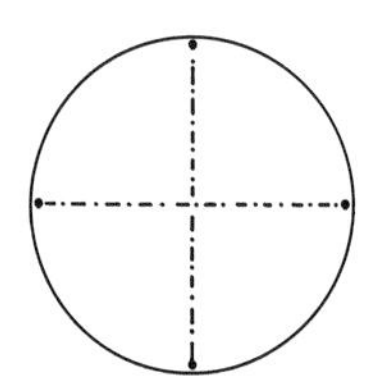

5. Unfold circle. Place dot precisely at each end of new folding line on front and back of circle.

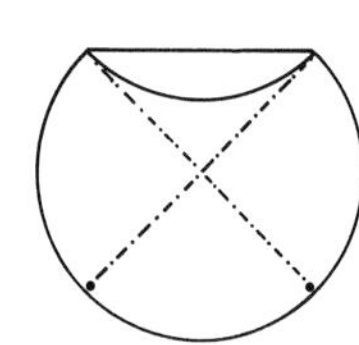

6. Rotate circle so folding lines form X. Fold top edge of circle between two dots to create one edge of square.

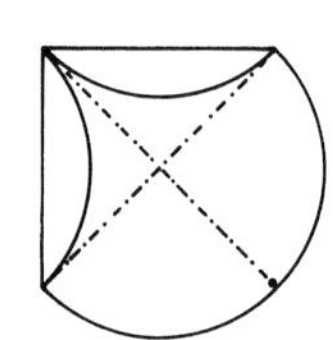

7. Rotate circle and fold next edge between two dots to make another edge of square.

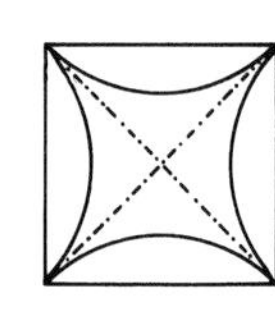

8. Continue rotating circle and folding edges until square is formed.

Santa Projects

Santa's smiling face is the choice for this quick-to-make gift tag, which can double as a tree ornament, a holiday greeting, or both! Untie the bow and you can tuck him inside an envelope and send him on his way.

Materials

For one 5″ (12.7 cm) card

Patterns on page 112

Equipment in work box, pages 4–6

5″ (12.7 cm) square of white paper

3½″ (8.9 cm) square of red paper

2″ (5.1 cm) square of pink paper

1″ (2.5 cm) square of black paper

Paper punch, ⅛″ (0.3 cm) diameter

12″ (30.5 cm) piece of narrow green ribbon or string

Red fine-line marker

Envelope, 4⅛″ × 5½″ (10.5 cm × 14.0 cm), or Envelope A pattern, page 82, and instructions, pages 80–82

Instructions

1. Trace or photocopy patterns, transferring all markings. Cut out. Carefully cut face from beard and reserve for use as face pattern. Punch out eye dots and hat dot trim.
2. Using craft knife on protected work surface, score and fold white paper in half diagonally. Align "place on fold" edge of pattern along folded edge of paper. Anchor with tape or paper clips and draw around shape. Transfer face placement and mouth line. Cut out head.
3. Mark one hat with trim on red paper. Cut out hat and punch out dot trim. On pink paper, draw one face, transferring position of eyes. Punch out two eyes from black paper and glue in place on face. Glue face and hat to head. Draw mouth on beard. Insert ribbon in hat hole and tie it in a bow.

Ornament Cards

Fold a paper star or weave a quilt-block wreath for this Christmas greeting. Each ornament, complete with hanging loop, lifts from its card to brighten a winter window or embellish a holiday tree.

Materials

For one 4¼″ × 5½″ (10.8 cm × 14.0 cm) card

Equipment in work box, pages 4-6

5½″ × 8½″ (14.0 cm × 21.6 cm) piece of sturdy paper

One completed wreath or star ornament (instructions follow)

One silver self-sticking star

Silver felt-tip pen, optional

Envelope, 4⅜″ × 5¾″ (11.1 cm × 14.6 cm), or Envelope B pattern, page 82, and instructions, pages 80-82

Instructions

1. Score and fold 5½″ × 8½″ (14.0 cm × 21.6 cm) piece of paper crosswise. Use felt-tip pen to add narrow silver border to card if desired.
2. On center top edge of card front, cut ¼″ (0.6 cm) slot. Center ornament on card front and slide monofilament hanging loop of ornament into slot. On reverse side of card front use self-sticking star to hold monofilament hanging loop in place.

Woven Wreath Ornament

Two scored and folded paper strips are intertwined with each other to make this Woven Wreath Ornament. For best results use stationery-weight paper and press the finished ornament in a heavy book for a day or two after you have finished making it.

Instructions

1. Photocopy or trace pattern with markings and cut out. Pierce folding lines in several places with pin.
2. Tape or clip pattern on one color paper strip. Draw slanted ends of pattern shape. Place pencil dots in pinholes to transfer folding lines.
3. Remove pattern and trim slanted ends on pattern lines with craft knife. Score folding lines. Repeat steps 2 and 3 with remaining paper strip.

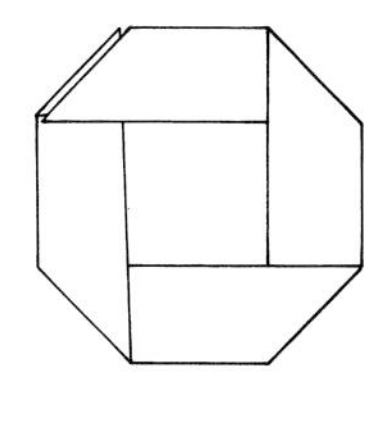

1. To make wreath ornament, fold and glue strip 1 to form ring, placing glue tab between layers.

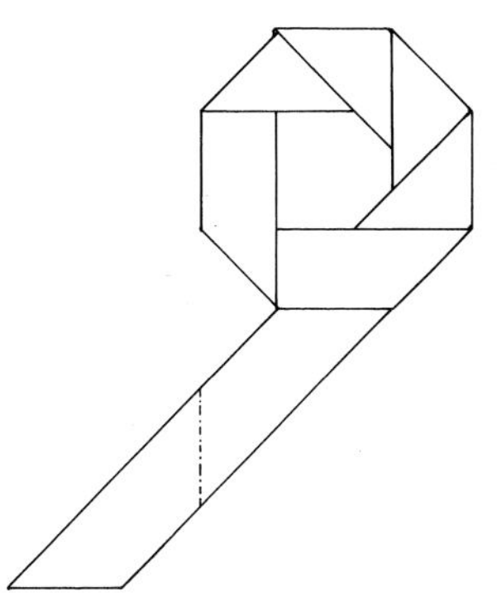

2. Fold glue tab of strip 2 over top of folded strip 1. Fold and weave strip 2 around strip 1.

Materials

For one 3½″ (8.9 cm) diameter wreath ornament

Pattern on page 113

Equipment in work box, pages 4–6

Two 1″ × 11¼″ (2.5 cm × 28.6 cm) strips of contrasting color paper, each strip same color on both sides

6″ (15.2 cm) length of monofilament for hanging loop

4. Refer to Drawing 1 to fold strip 1, creating squarish ring. Add glue to tab and hold until dry.
5. Fold remaining strip 2 in same way, but do not glue it. Unfold strip 2. Referring to Drawing 2, wrap and weave strip 2 around folded and glued strip 1. Start by folding unglued tab of strip 2 over top edge of folded and glued strip 1 ring. Weave and wrap strip 2 around ring, passing end of strip 2 through center of ring. When end of strip 2 reaches glue tab of strip 2, glue them together with hanging loop sandwiched between them.

Folded Star

A single strip of paper can be quickly folded into a star ornament. For best results the paper strip should be the same color or the same pattern on both sides. Two same-sized strips of lightweight gift wrap can be glued together, back to back, to make a double-faced patterned paper for this project. Removable tape serves as an extra pair of hands, keeping the star precisely folded and attached to the folding guide until the layers of the star are glued together.

Materials

For one 3¾″ (9.5 cm) diameter star ornament

Photocopy of placement guide, page 113

Equipment in work box, pages 4–6

8″ × 10″ (20.4 cm × 25.4 cm) scrap of cardboard

⅝″ × 20½″ (1.6 cm × 52.1 cm) strip of paper

6″ (15.2 cm) length of monofilament for hanging loop

Instructions

1. Tape or glue trimmed folding guide onto cardboard and then tape guide to work surface.
2. Referring to Drawings 1 through 5, tape paper strip in place directly on folding guide as you fold and weave star. At each folded star tip use one piece of tape to hold strip on guide and one piece of tape to attach paper strip to itself, as in Drawing 1. Although not pictured on every drawing, tape should be used in this way on each star tip.

3. When star is nearly completed, as in Drawing 4, remove tape from extended tail at beginning. Fold down tail and tuck it into star overlapped area to conceal ending as in Drawing 5.
4. Remove tape at star tips only. Tie monofilament hanging loop at star top. Place dots of glue (designated with circles on Drawing 6) between paper layers at every overlapped area of star, including tips. Remove all tape.

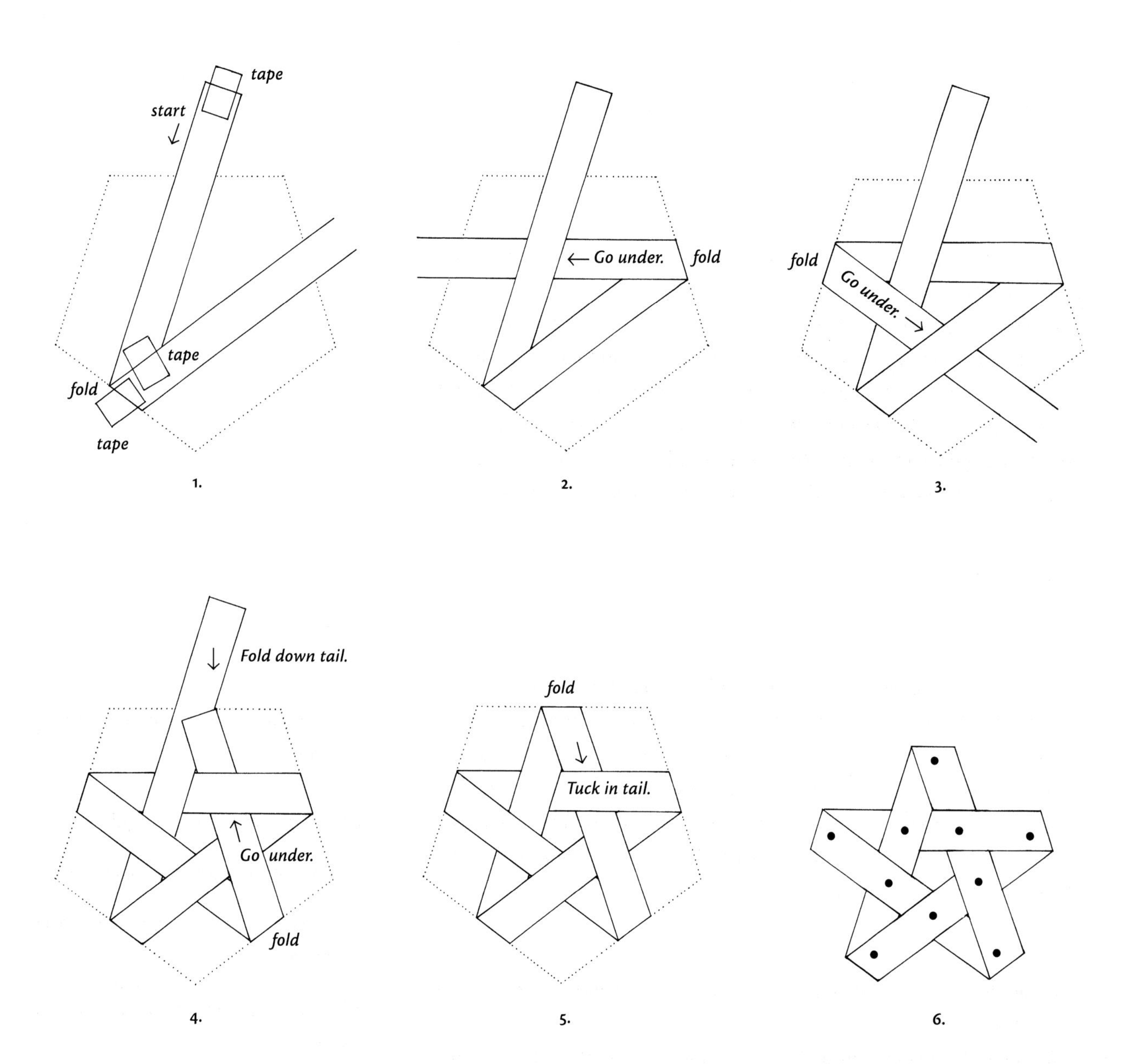

Garland of Snowmen Card

A line of velour top hats crowns this chorus of six snowmen. Select opaque white paper for the snowmen so their black hats will not show through and darken their smiling faces. If the paper is rather thick, fold and cut only two or three figures at a time. Use paper punches to make buttons and faces, or draw them with felt-tip pens.

Instructions

1. Trace or photocopy patterns, transferring placement lines and all details onto each one. Cut out patterns. On snowmen, use paper punches to cut out cheeks, eyes, and buttons. Pierce mouth dots with needle.
2. Use light pencil lines to divide 10½″ (26.4 cm) length of white paper at six 1¾″ (4.4 cm) intervals. Score and accordion-fold paper to make piece 1¾″ × 3″ (4.4 cm × 7.7 cm). Crease all folding lines sharply.
3. Place snowman pattern on folded paper. Side edges of pattern should touch folded edges of paper. Tape or clip pattern to paper, draw around shape, and remove pattern.
4. Anchor folded paper layers together with tape or paper clips. Using craft knife on protected work surface, cut out snowman shape. Unfold garland. Hold snowman pattern against each figure and mark placement of eyes, cheeks, and buttons.

Materials

For one 3³⁄₁₆″ × 10½″ (8.1 cm × 26.7 cm) garland

Patterns on page 114

Equipment in work box, pages 4–6

3″ × 10½″ (7.7 cm × 26.4 cm) piece of white paper

2″ × 10½″ (5.1 cm × 26.4 cm) piece of black paper

Six pieces of ¼″ × 3⅛″ (0.6 cm × 8.0 cm) colored paper for scarves

Small scraps of black and pale pink paper

Paper punches, ⅛″ (0.3 cm) and ¼″ (0.6 cm) diameters

Envelope, 3⅝″ × 6½″ (9.2 cm × 16.5 cm), or Envelope D pattern, page 83, and instructions, pages 80–83

5. To make hat garland, divide 10½″ (26.4 cm) length of black paper at six 1¾″ (4.4 cm) intervals. If using velour paper, make marks on reverse side. Score and accordion-fold paper to make unit 1¾″ × 2″ (4.4 cm × 5.1 cm). Crease all folding lines sharply.
6. Place hat pattern on folded paper. Side edges of pattern should touch folded edges of paper. Tape or clip pattern to paper, draw around shape, transferring slot line, and remove pattern.
7. Anchor folded paper layers together with tape or paper clips. Cut out hat and slot. Unfold garland. Make sure all slots are cut. Slide hats over head tops, aligning top edge of each hat slot with placement line on head. Glue in place. Punch out black buttons and eyes and pink cheeks. Glue in place on snowmen.
8. Use scarf pattern to mark placement of folding line, fringes, and slots on paper strips. Transfer these pattern details to scarf papers with pin pricks. Cut fringes and slots. Place each scarf on neck of snowman and interlock slots. Unfold a few snowmen so envelope will not be too thick.

6

Envelopes & Patterns

Making Envelopes

Materials

For one envelope A, B, C, D, or E

Pattern size of your choice, pages 82, 83, and 84

Equipment in work box, pages 4-6

Paper of your choice (size requirements listed on each pattern)

Once you have drawn the patterns, creating your own envelopes is truly a quick and easy task. It's also fun because of the unlimited choices of color, texture, and size. Patterns and illustrated instructions are provided here for making five envelope sizes. To make an envelope of a different size, carefully lift the glued flap of an existing envelope, open the folds, and use the flattened envelope as a pattern to create others. Glue your envelope patterns to acetate to extend their lives.

In order to be acceptable for mailing, envelopes must conform to certain postal standards regarding minimum size, proper height-to-length ratio, and maximum thickness of contents. To avoid postal surcharges as well as delivery delays due to returned unacceptable envelopes, visit your post office and request information about current standards or ask for a photocopy of the template that clerks use to check mail dimensions. At the time of writing, all the envelopes in this book meet the United States Postal Service requirements.

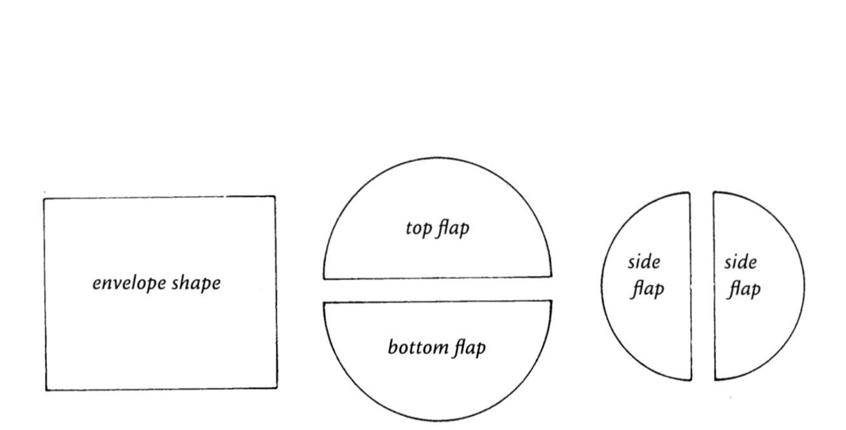

1. Trace rectangular envelope pattern in size of your choice. Also make two tracings of semicircular top and bottom flap and two tracings of semicircular side flap. For greatest accuracy, use compass to trace semicircles. Cut out all pattern pieces.

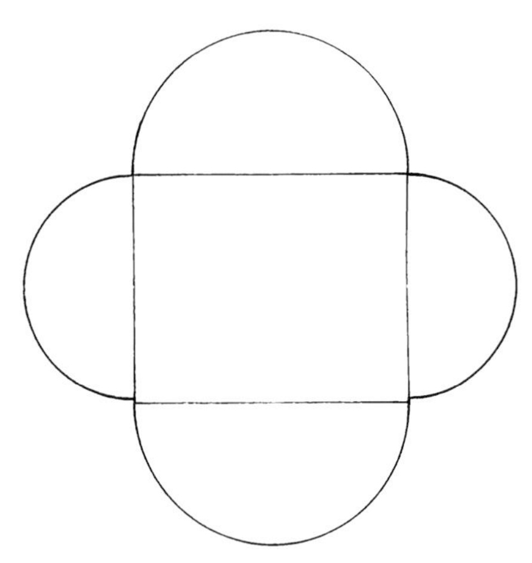

2. Arrange pattern pieces in proper order on work surface and tape them together. Practice folding envelope pattern to check alignment of flaps.

3. Trace pattern for optional liner circle on folded paper and cut it out.

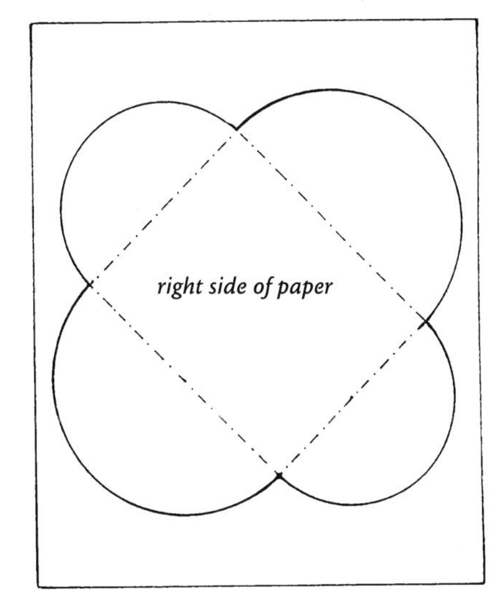

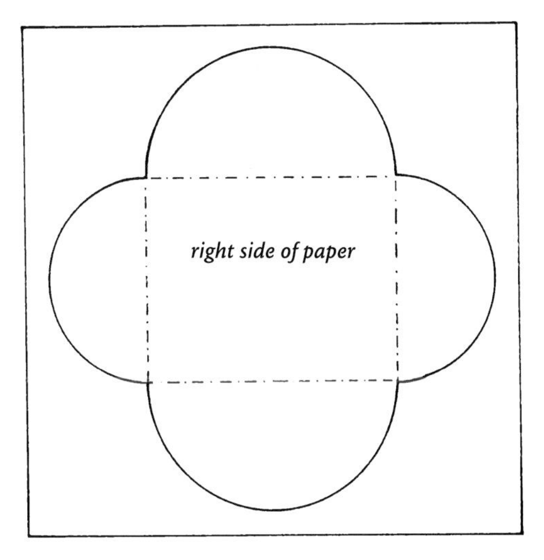

4. Place square or rectangle of selected paper right-side up on protected work surface. Tape or clip pattern onto paper and draw around pattern shape. Remove pattern. Draw and score perpendicular lines within outlined shape to define straight edges of envelope. Cut out shape.

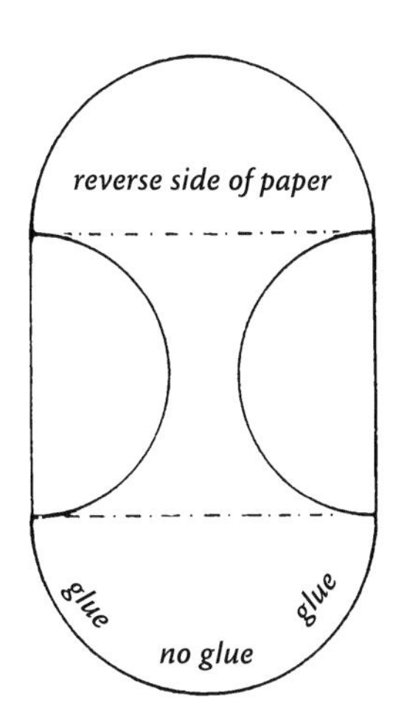

5. Flip envelope over to reverse side of paper. Fold in side flaps. Apply glue to edges of bottom flap, avoiding center area.

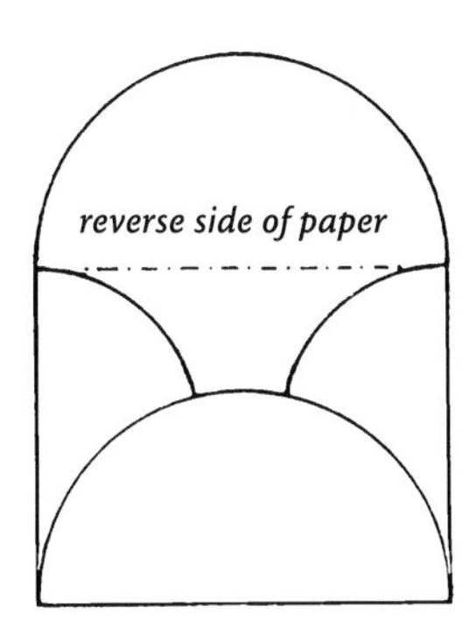

6. Fold up bottom flap so it overlaps side flaps. To protect interior of envelope from misplaced glue, slide in scrap piece of paper to keep front and back layers separated. Remove scrap paper just before glue is dry.

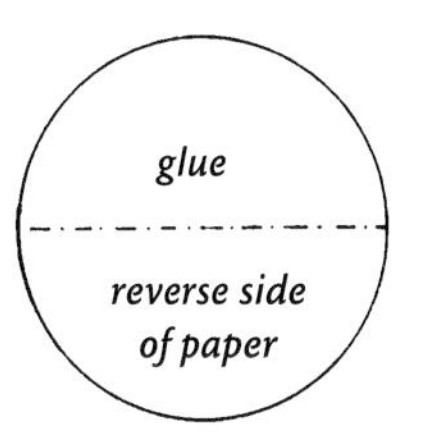

7. Flip optional liner over to reverse side and apply glue only to half of circle above folding line.

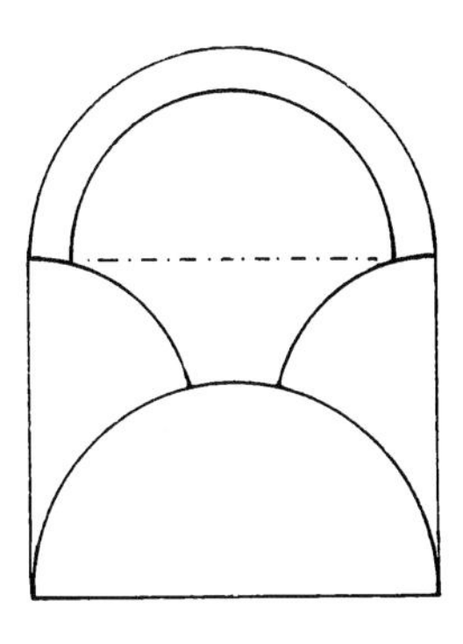

8. Slide unglued portion of liner inside envelope. Center glued area of liner on top flap, aligning folds, and press two layers together. Immediately fold down top flap to finalize placement of liner. In order to hinge well, folding lines of liner and envelope will probably shift and not be aligned after folding down and then lifting top flap. Insert card and seal envelope.

Envelopes A and B

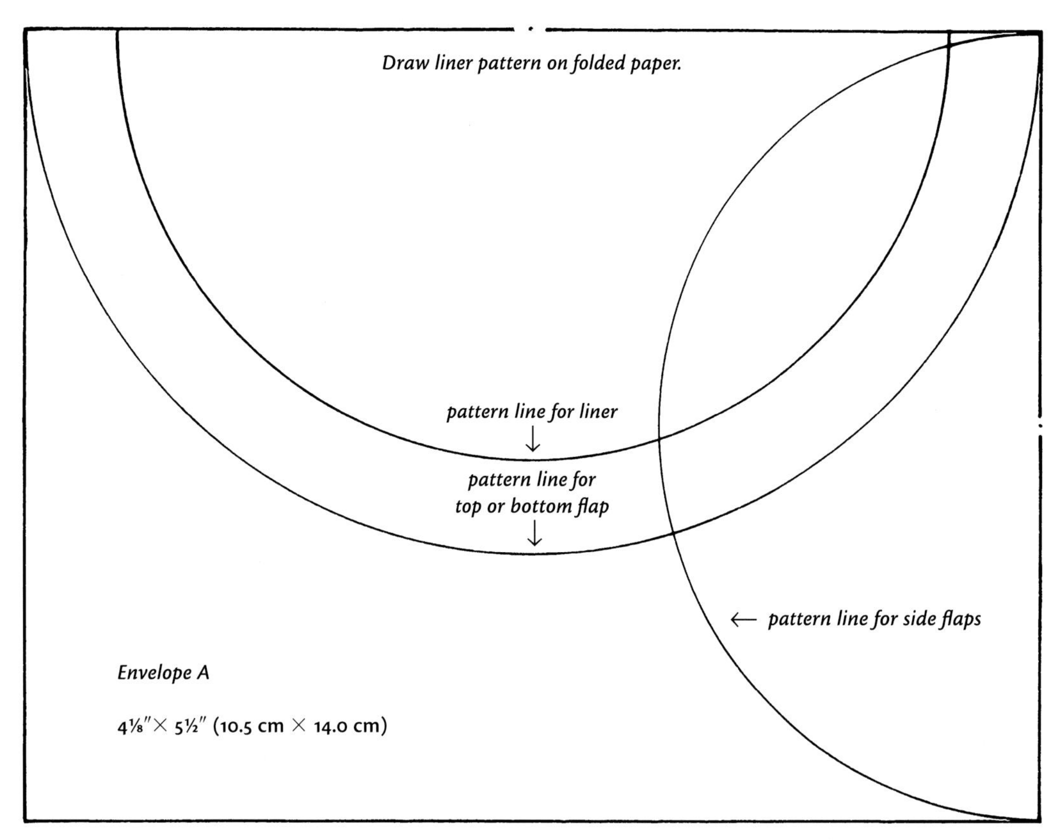

Envelope A: Refer to general directions for all envelopes and center complete pattern on 10″ (25.4 cm) square of paper or place diagonally on 8½″ × 11″ (21.6 cm × 27.9 cm) piece of paper.

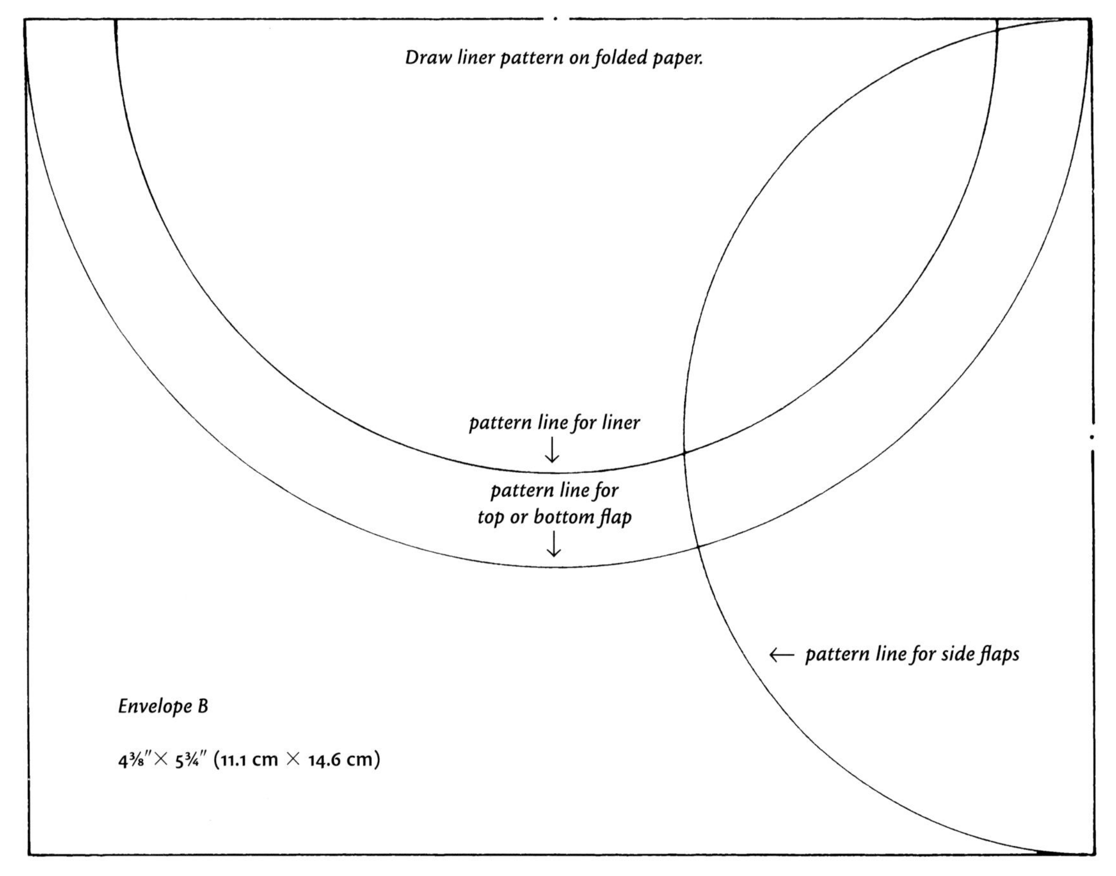

Envelope B: Refer to general directions for all envelopes and center complete pattern on 10½″ (26.7 cm) square of paper or place diagonally on 9″ × 12″ (22.8 cm × 30.5 cm) piece of paper.

Envelopes C and D

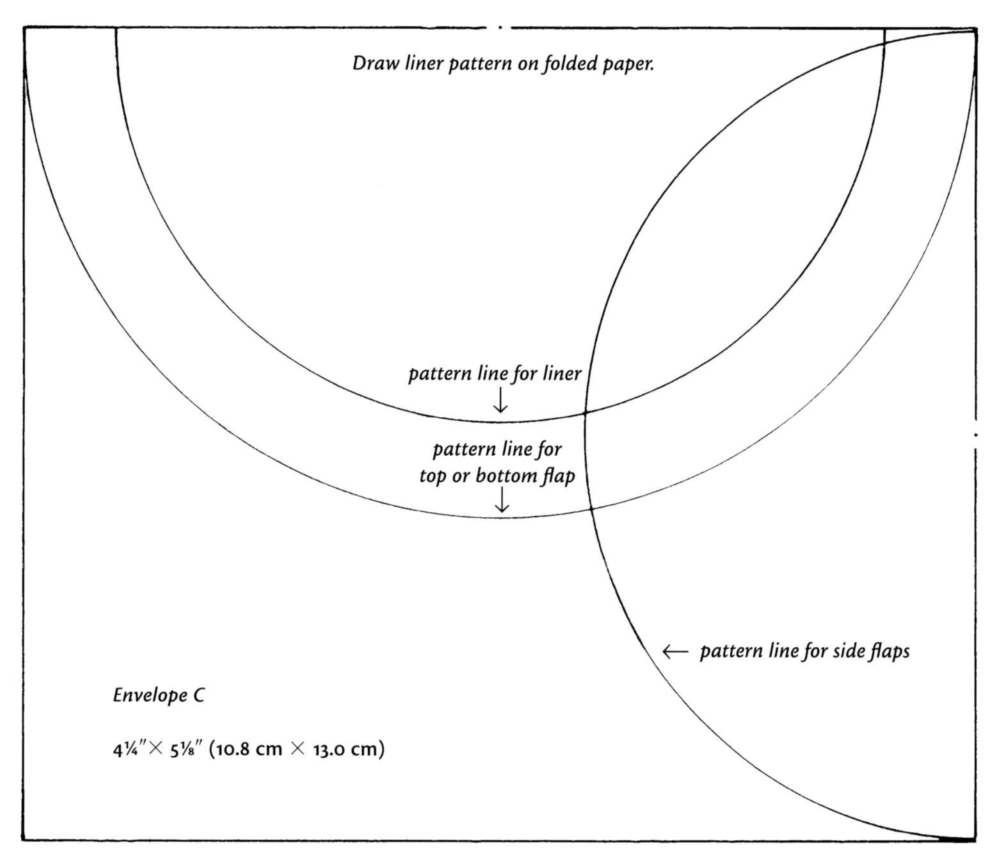

Envelope C: Refer to general directions for all envelopes and center complete pattern on 9¾″ (24.8 cm) square of paper or place diagonally on 8½″ × 11″ (21.6 cm × 27.9 cm) piece of paper.

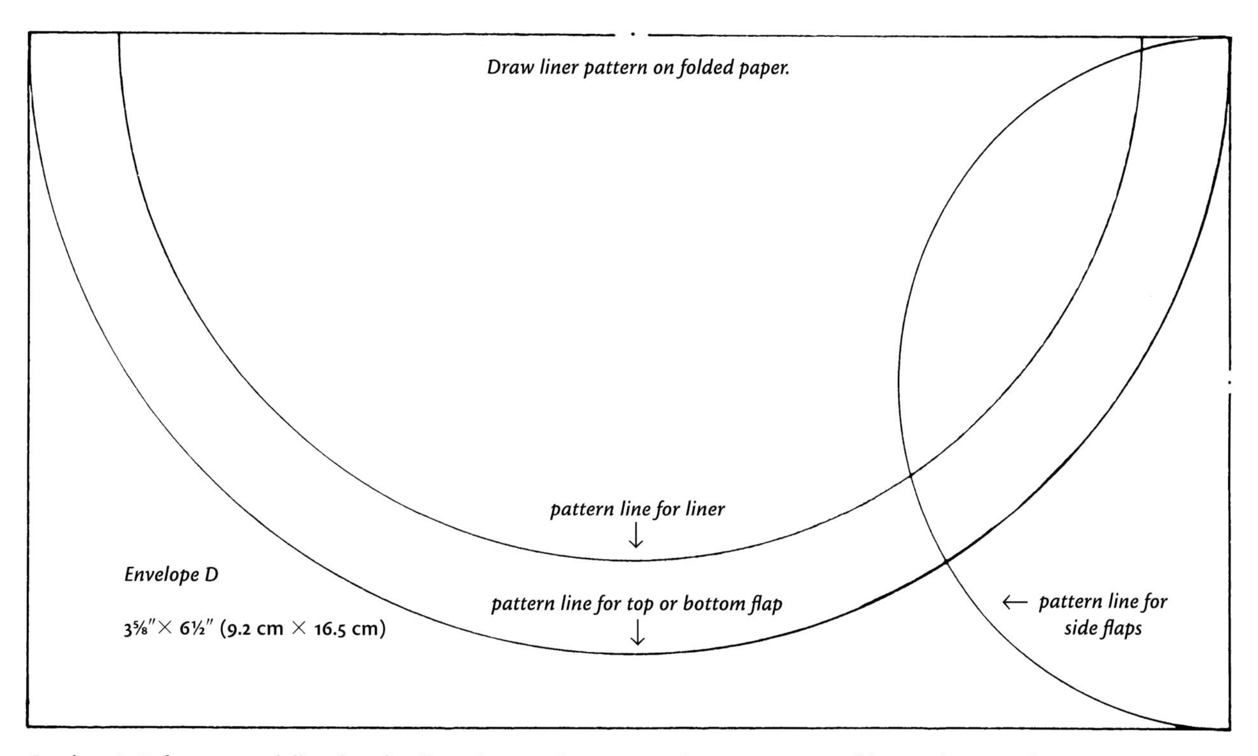

Envelope D: Refer to general directions for all envelopes and center complete pattern on 10½″ (26.7 cm) square of paper or place diagonally on 9″ × 12″ (22.8 cm × 30.5 cm) piece of paper.

Envelope E

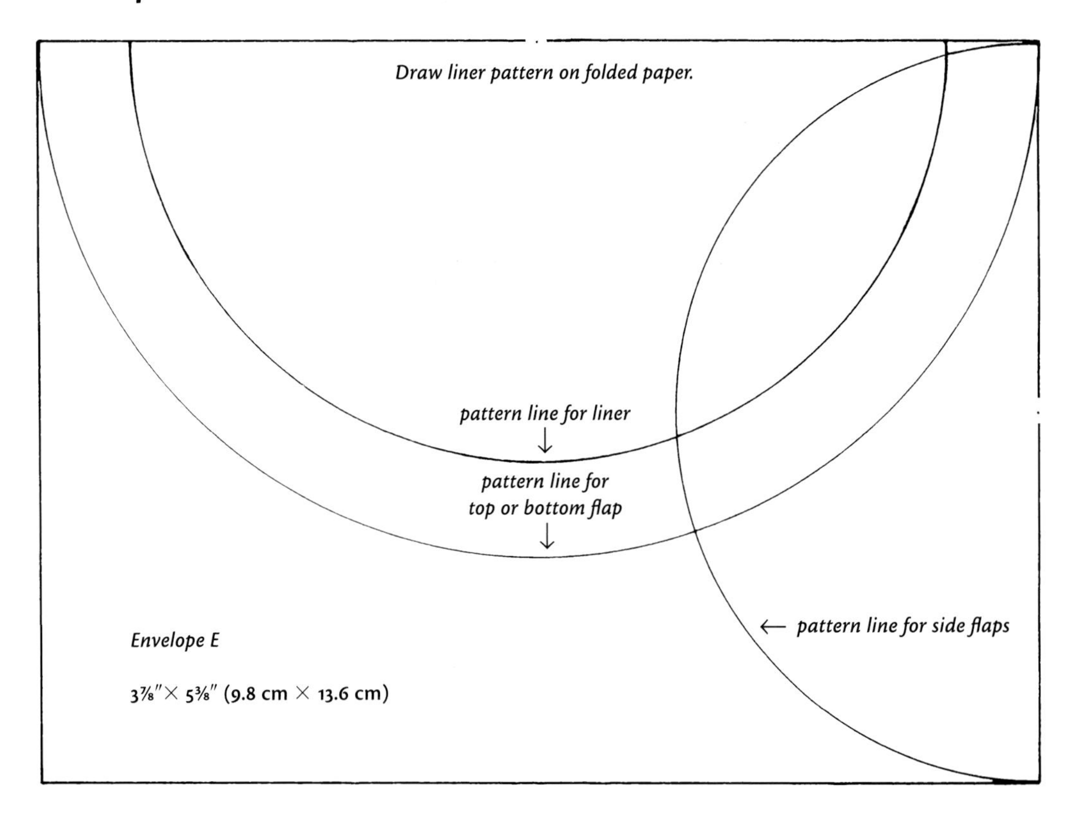

Envelope E: Refer to general directions for all envelopes and center complete pattern on 9½″ (24.1 cm) square of paper or place diagonally on 8½″ × 11″ (21.6 cm × 27.9 cm) piece of paper.

Kite Card and Tick-Tack-Toe Valentine

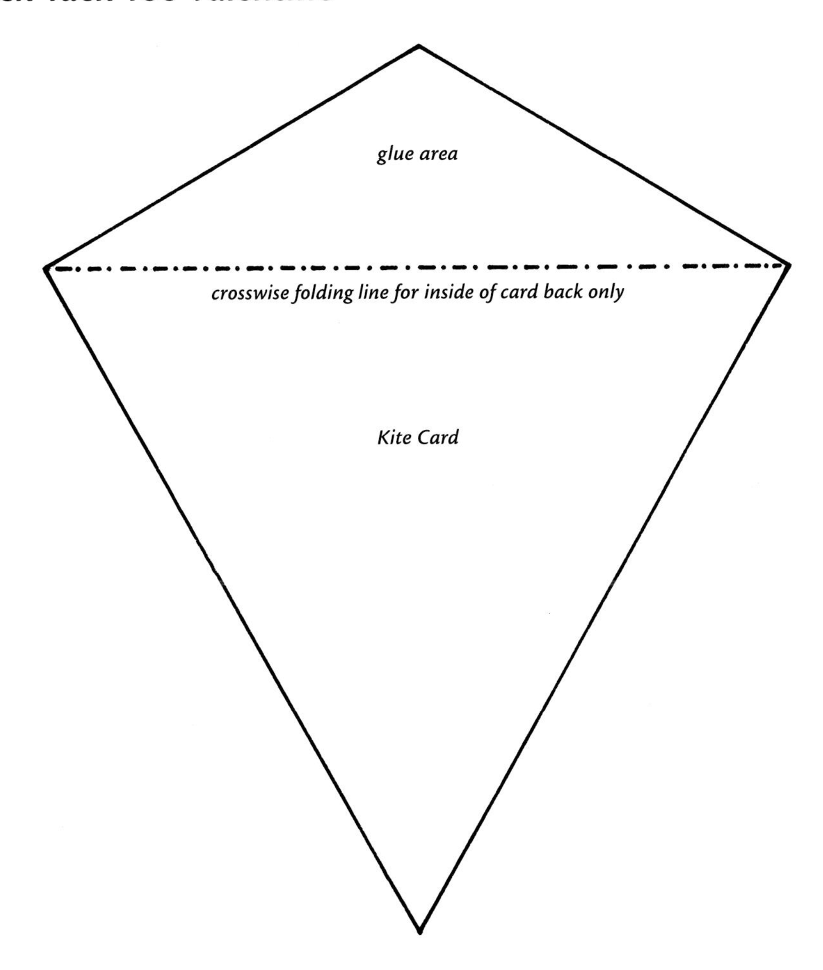

Folded Heart Card

Dove Note and Egg Bunny Card

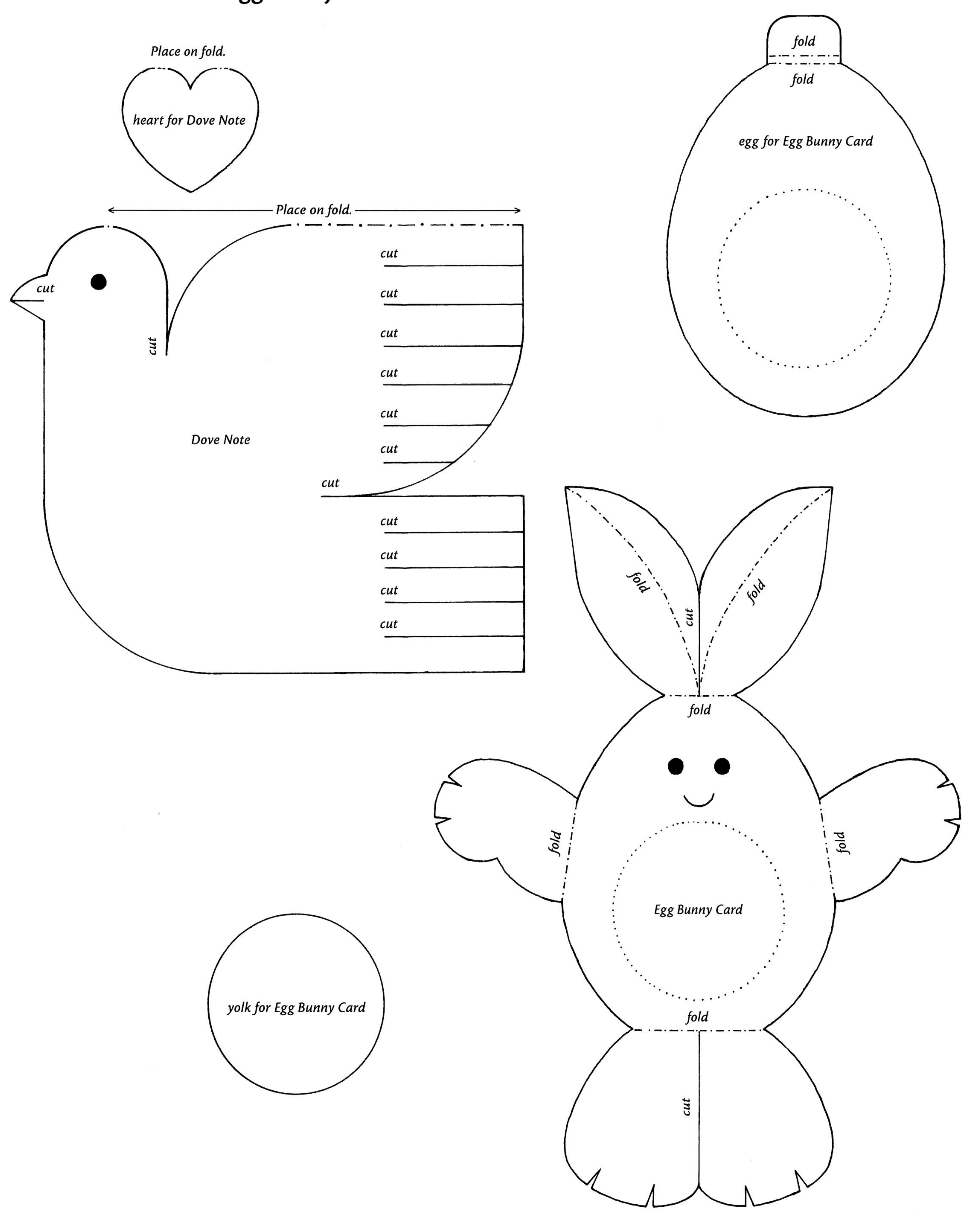

Leaf Cross Card

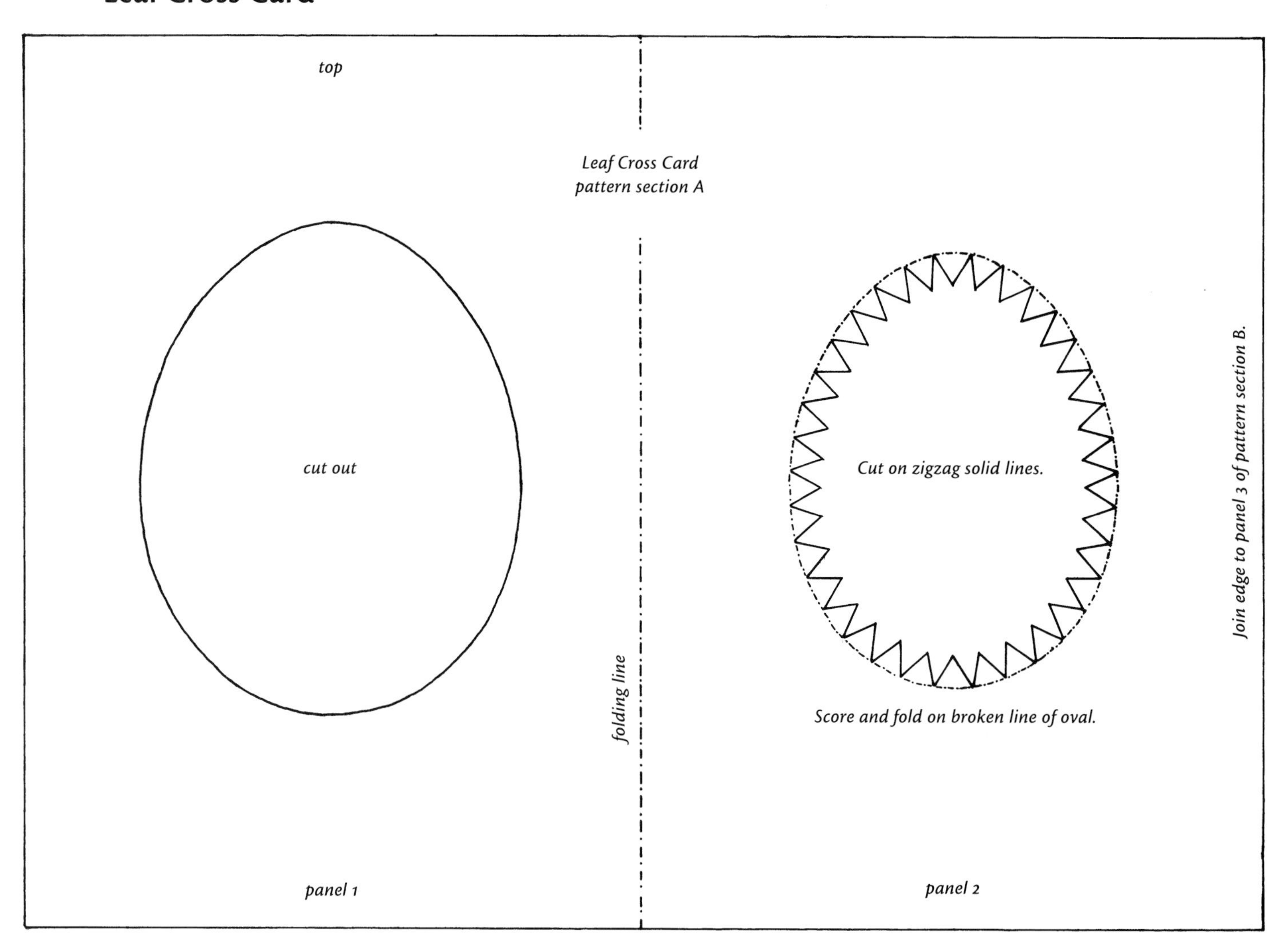

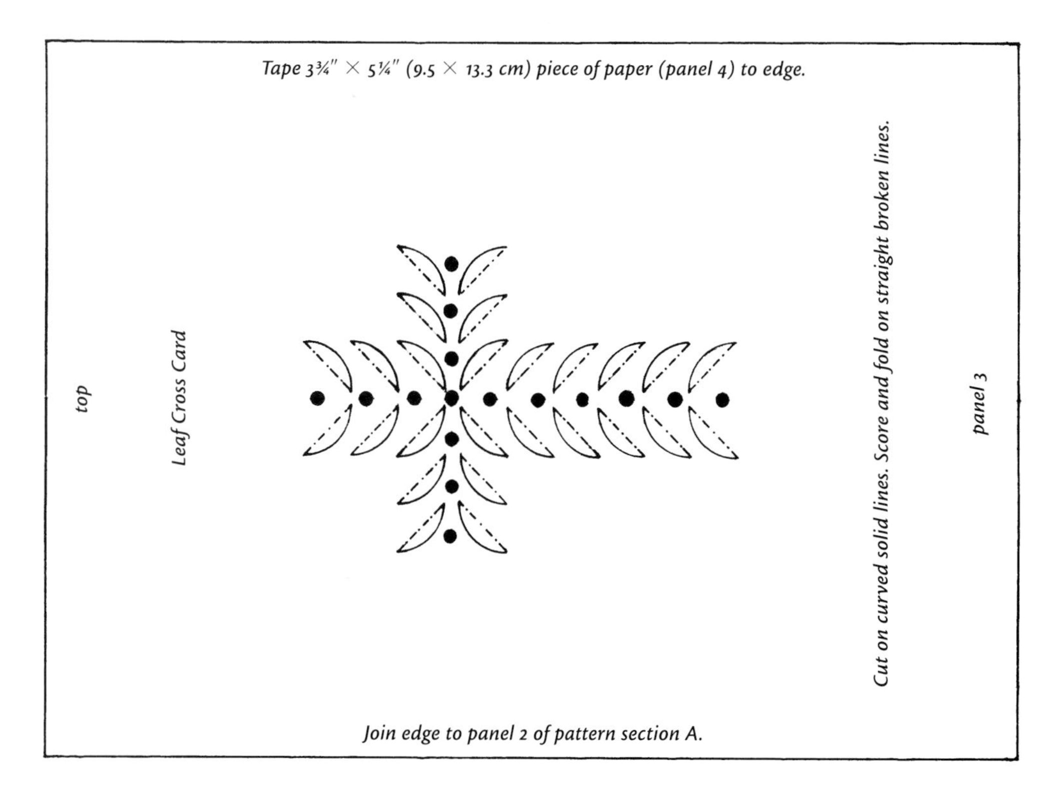

Tea for Two Cards and Duckling Designs

Baby Bib Announcement and Bassinet Card

glue tab B

top

ruffle for Bassinet Card

bottom

glue tab A

cut

teddy for Bassinet Card

cut

Glue tab B here.

Glue pleated ruffle here and top with colored strip.

bassinet for Bassinet Card

Glue color strip here.

Glue tab A here.

Place on fold.

Place on fold.

Baby Bib Announcement

Animal Note Cards

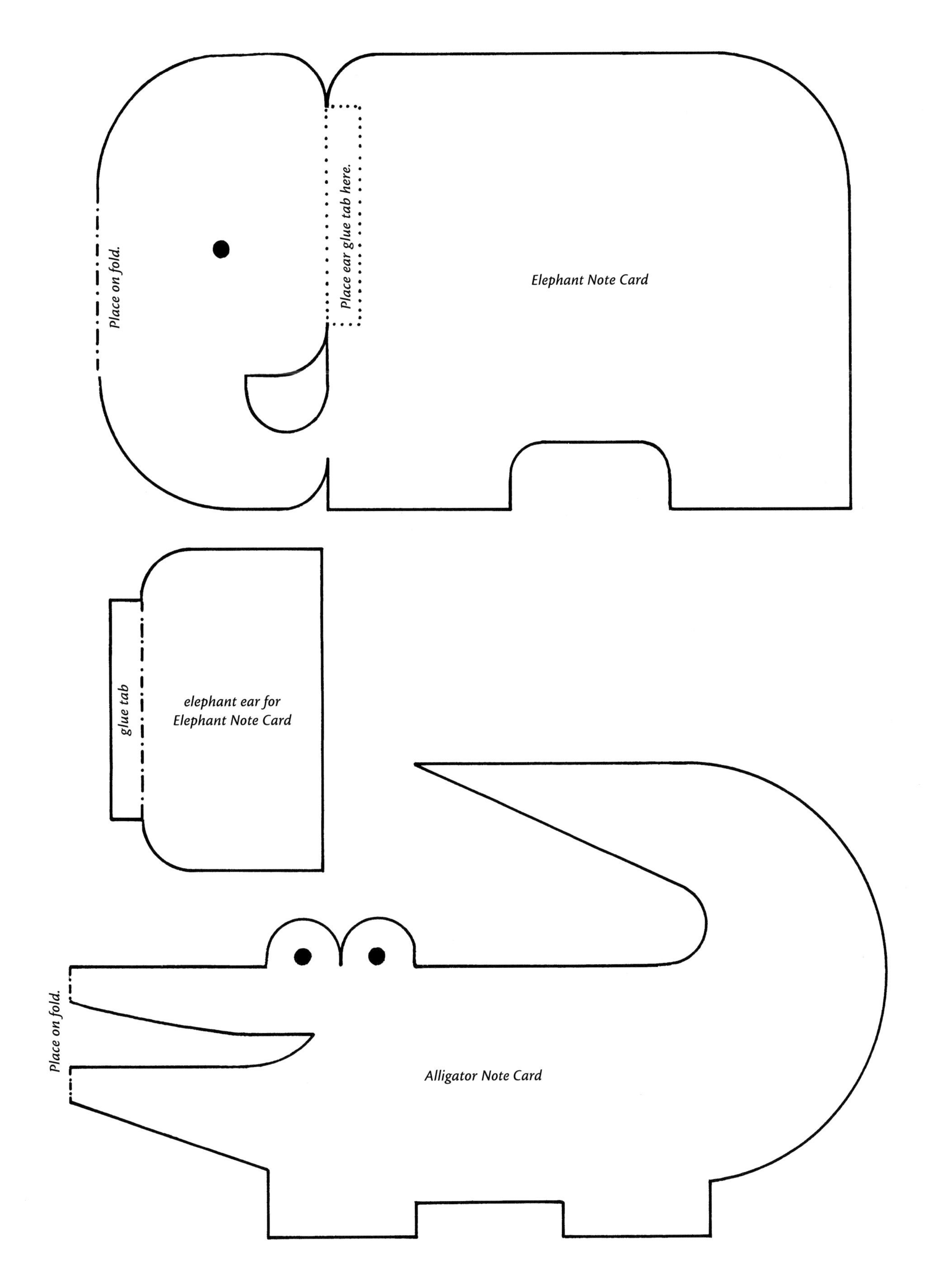

Animal Gift Tags and Piggy Bank Note

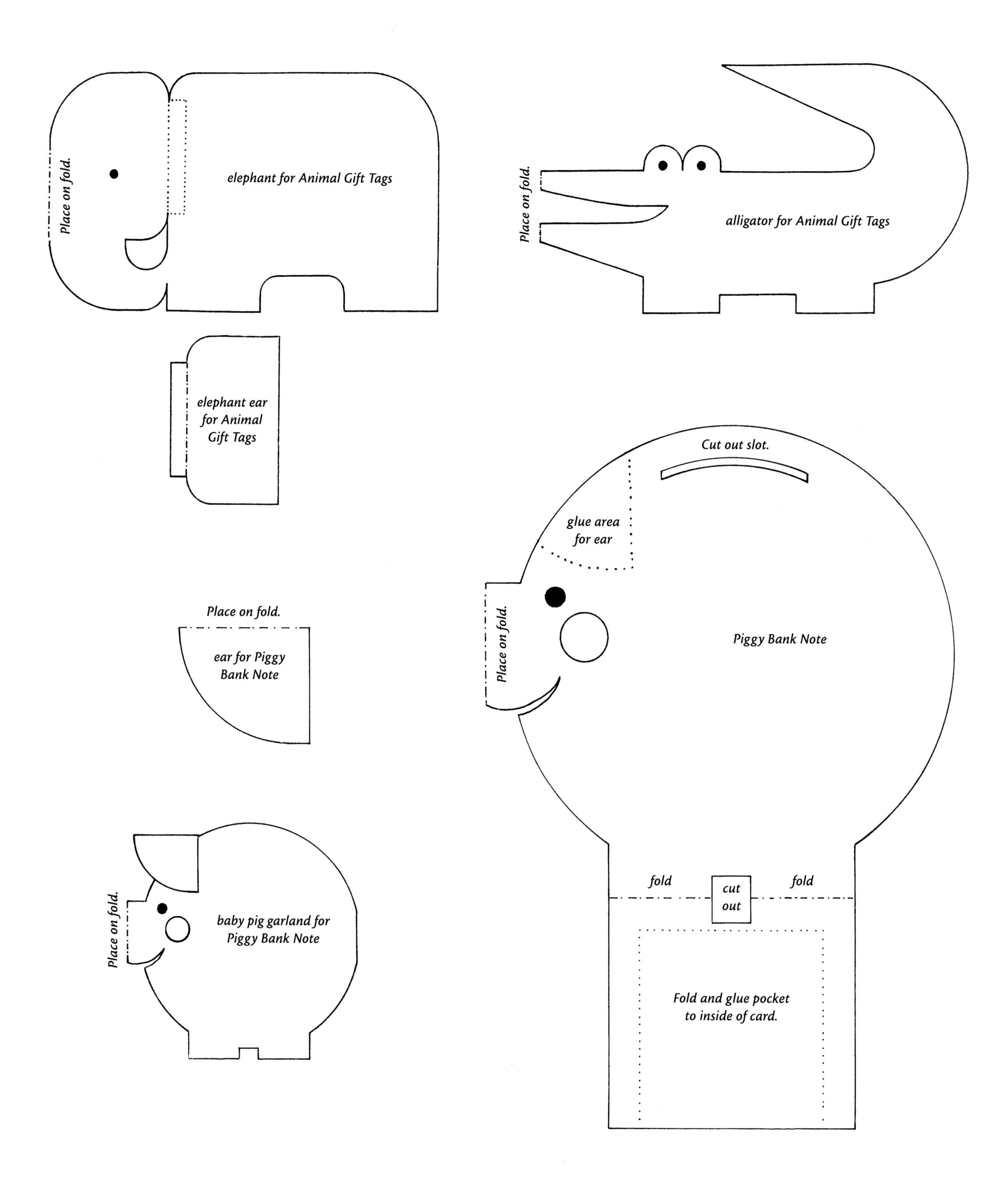

Sailboat Card

Keep glue close to edges.

top

water area for Sailboat Card

glue tab A
pocket 1
tier 1
pocket 2
tier 2
pocket 3
tier 3
pocket 4
tier 4
pocket 5
tier 5
glue tab B

V M V M V M V M V M M

Keep glue close to edges.

top

Sailboat Card

Top folded edge of pocket 1 rests ⅛" (0.3 cm) above this glue tab line.

↑ Cut edge of glue tab A goes here.

↑ Folded edge of glue tab A goes here.

Place on fold.

↑ Cut edge of glue tab B goes here. ↑

↓ Folded edge of glue tab B goes here. ↓

Pinwheel Card

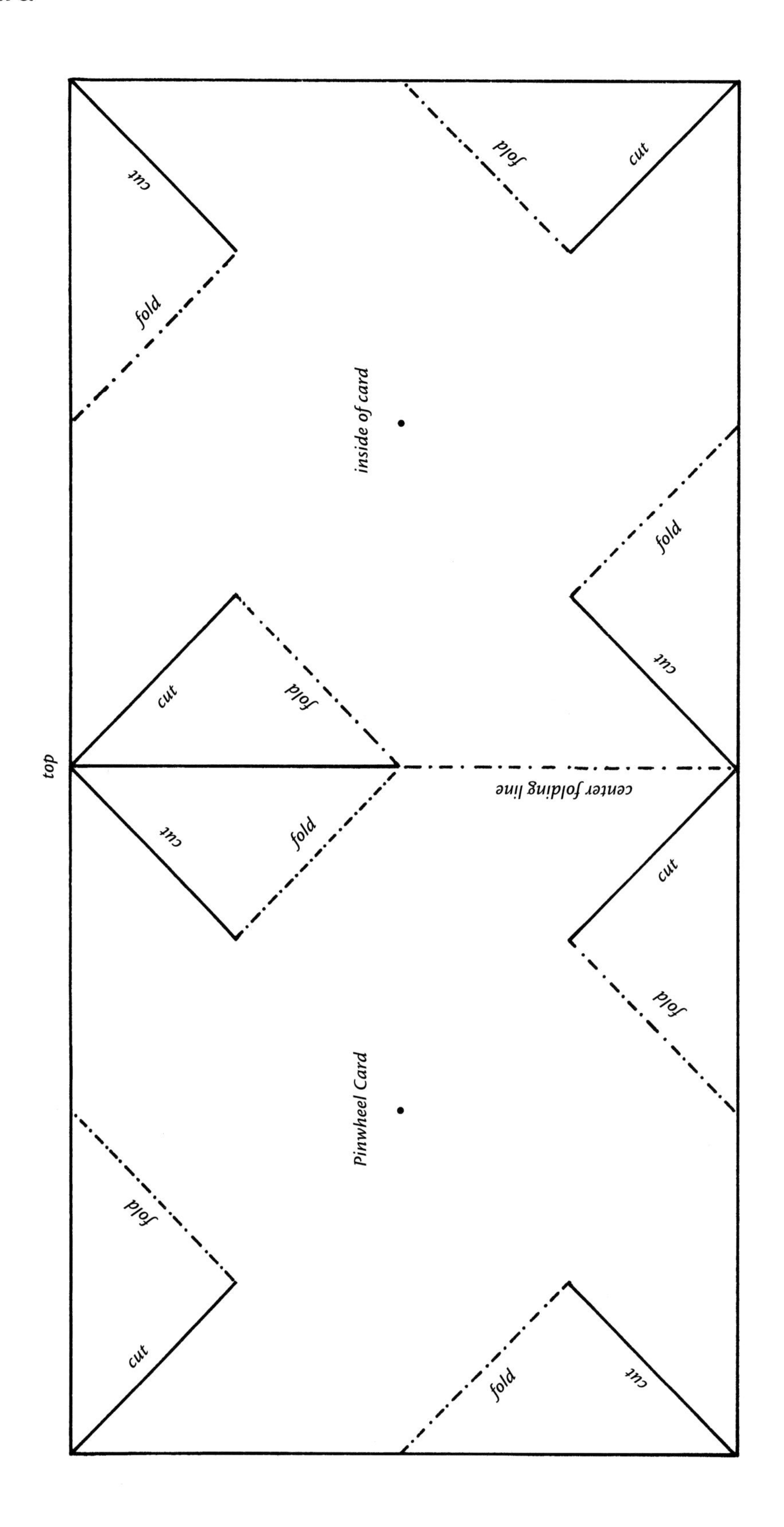

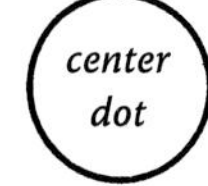

Tomato Pincushion Note and Paintbrush Note Card

tomato for Tomato Pincushion Note

C A

B B

A C

tomato calyx for Tomato Pincushion Note

Place on fold.

strawberry calyx for Tomato Pincushion Note

Place on fold.

strawberry for Tomato Pincushion Note

Punch out dot.

Paintbrush Note Card

When card is completed, cut fold to here. →

Place on fold.

Cut bristles on card front only.

Fish Note Card and Knife, Fork, and Spoon Invitation

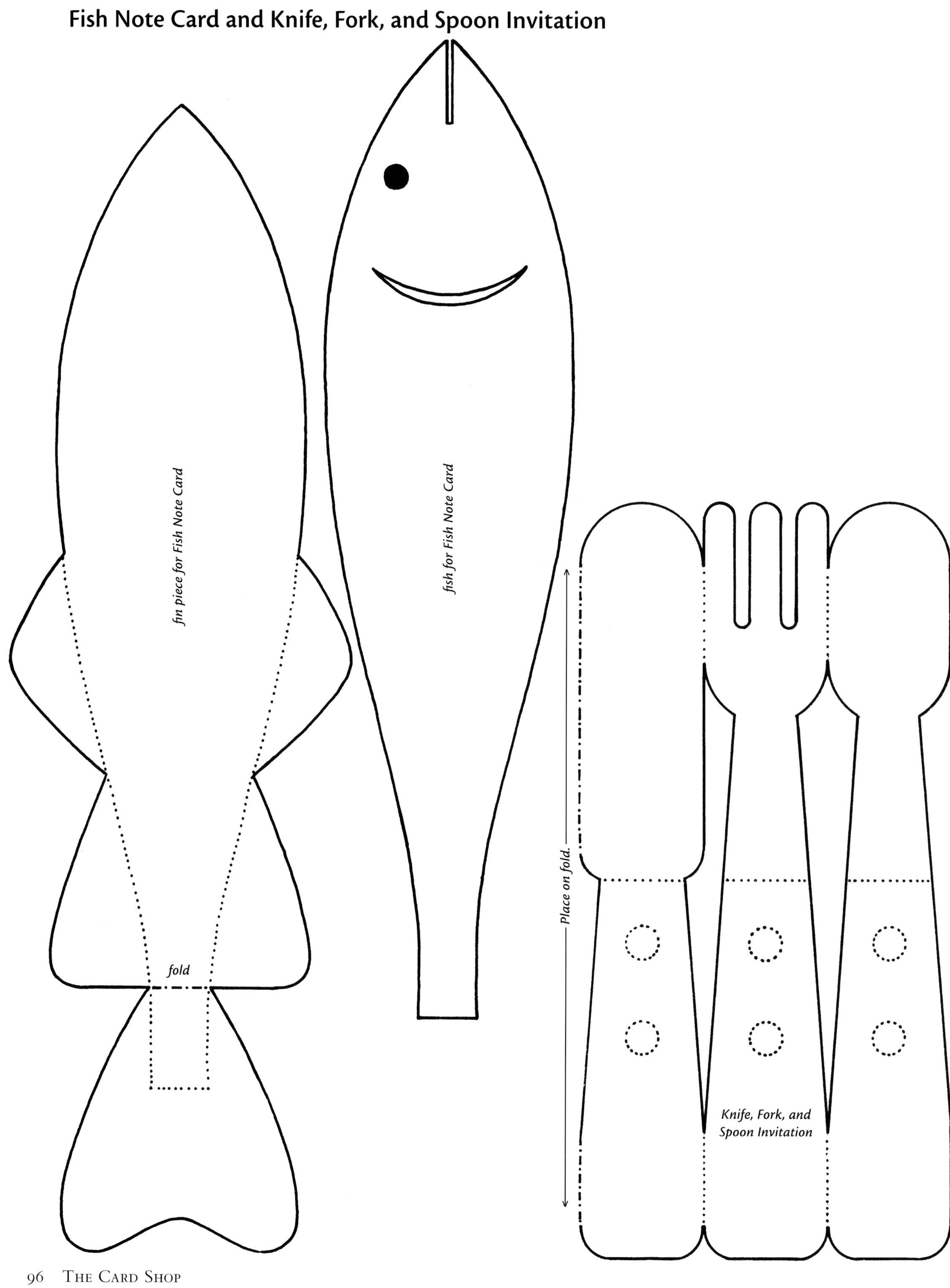

Hamburger Note Card

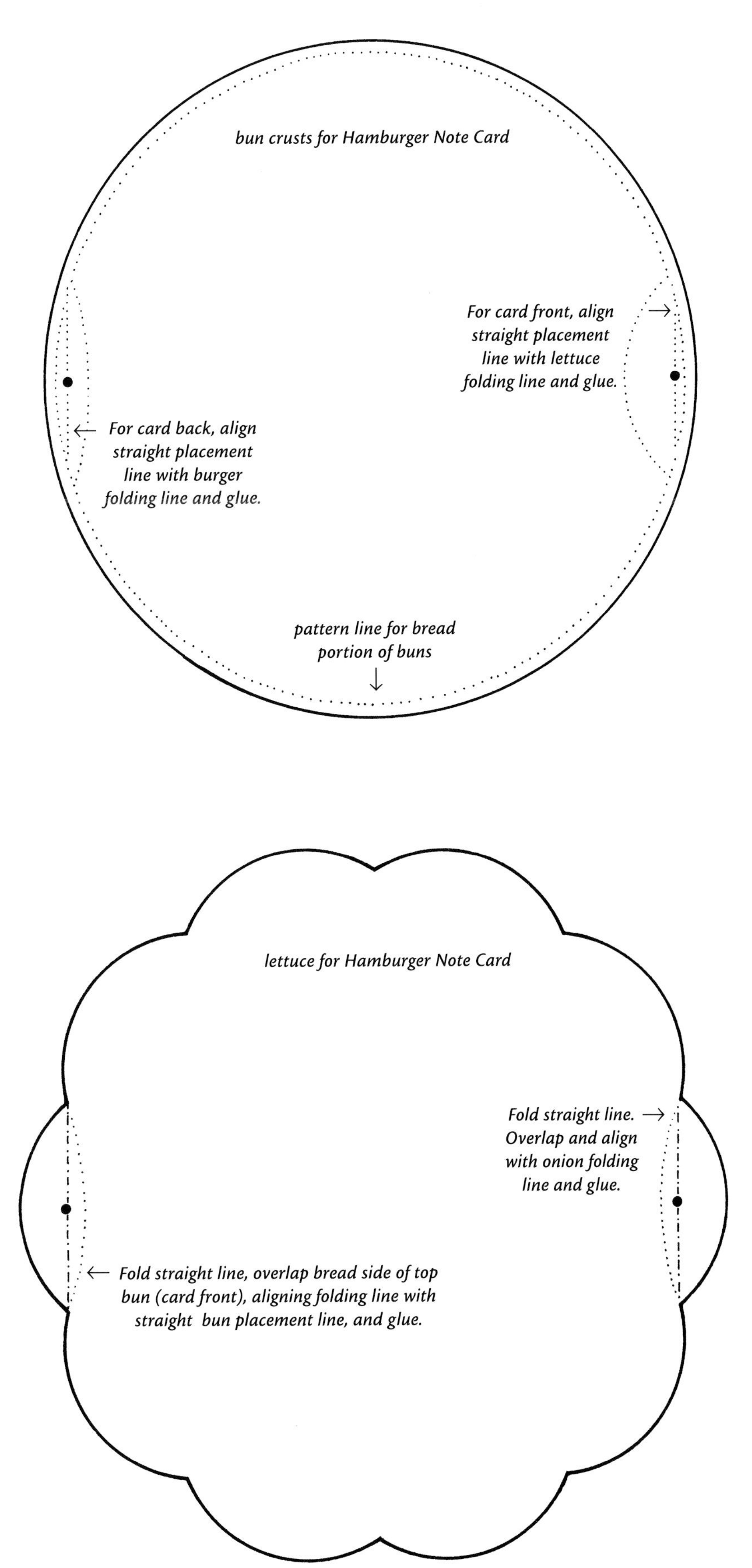

Hamburger Note Card (continued)

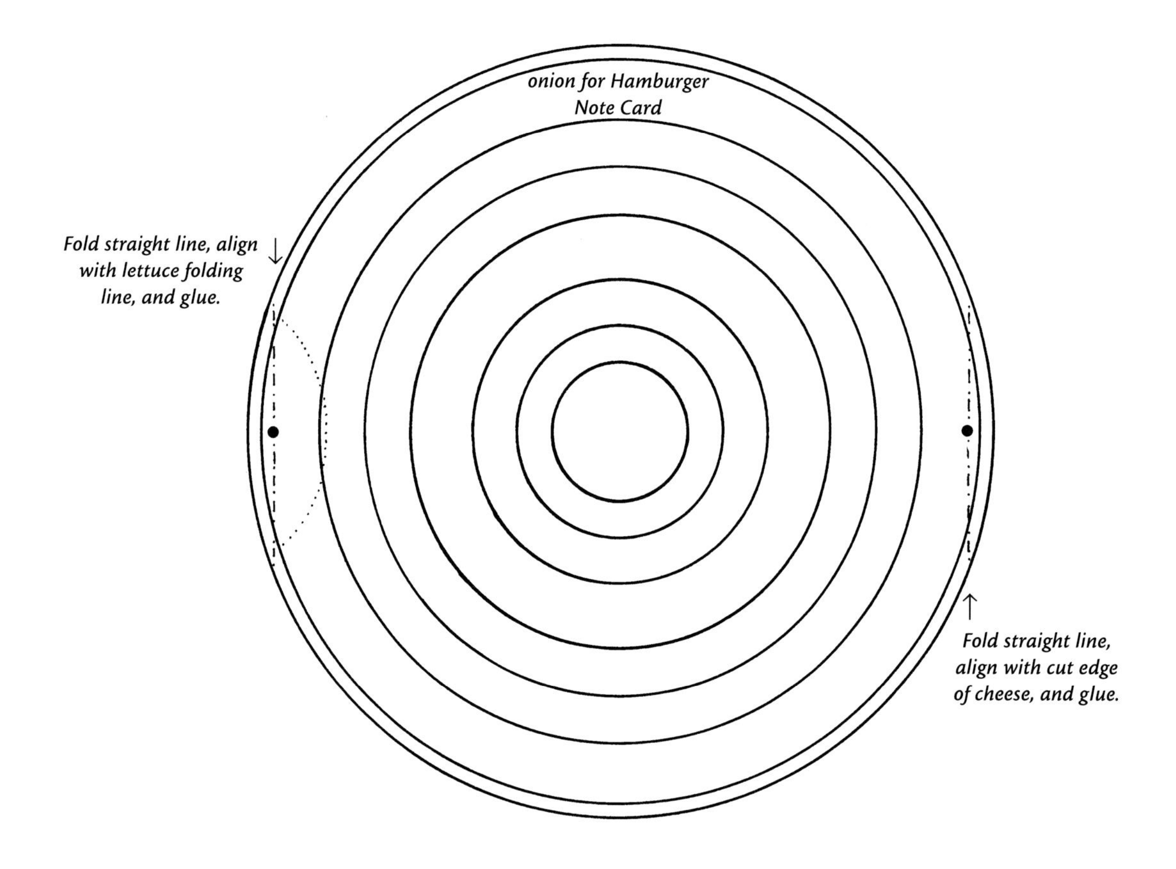

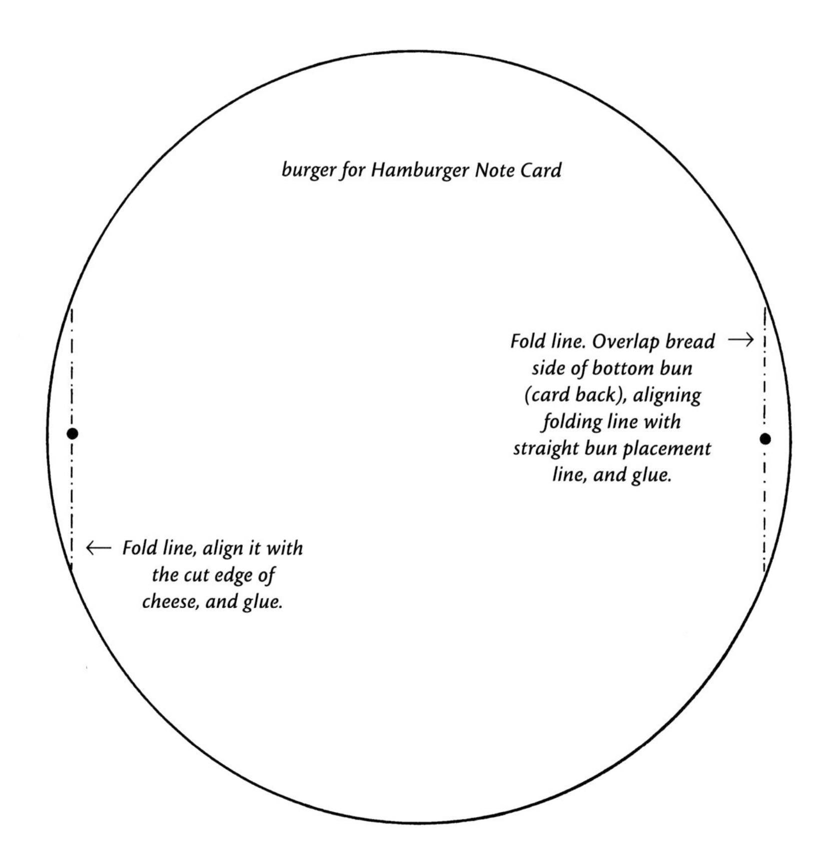

Pizza Note

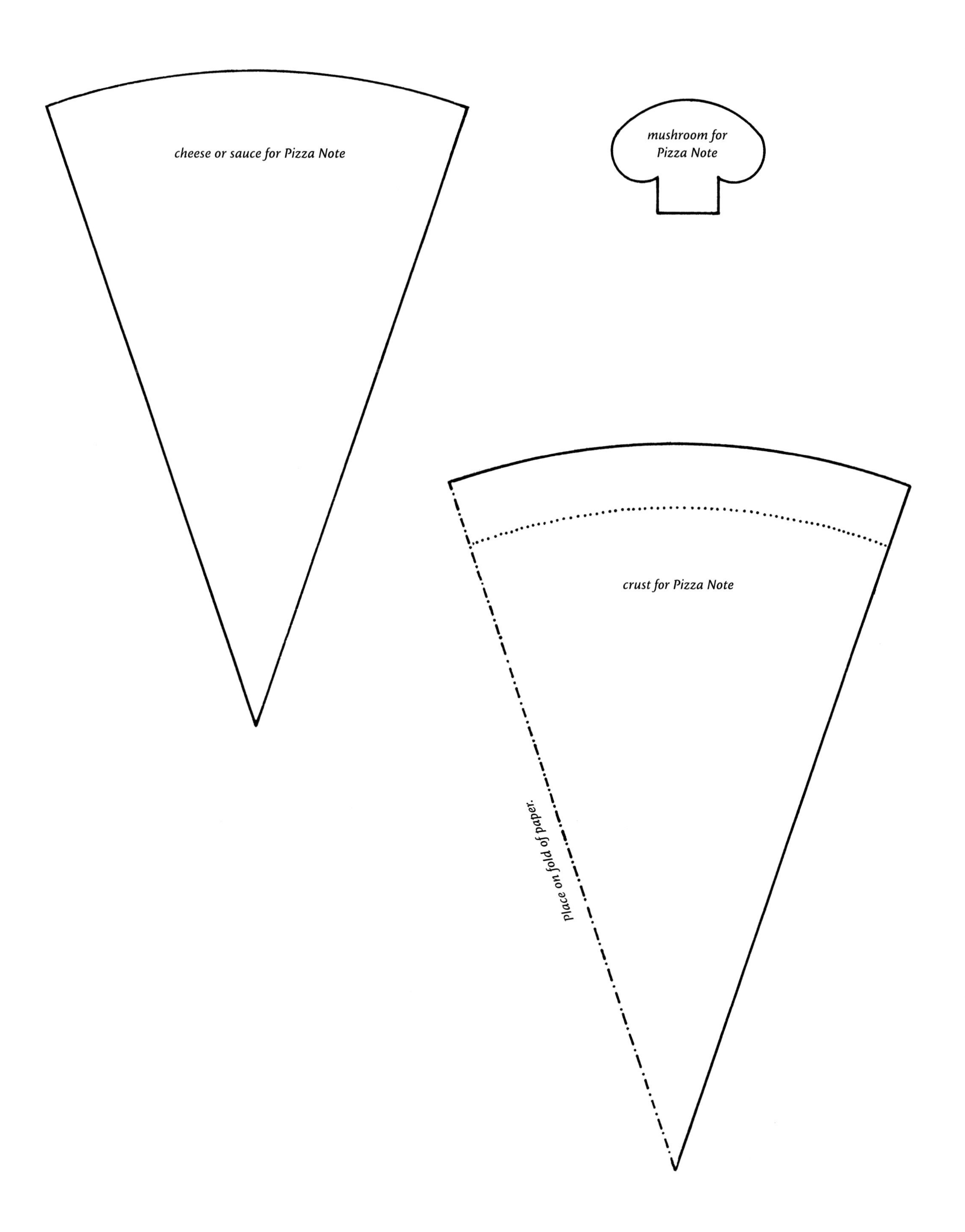

cheese or sauce for Pizza Note
mushroom for Pizza Note
crust for Pizza Note
Place on fold of paper.

Birthday Cupcake Card, Star Note Card, and Star Place Card

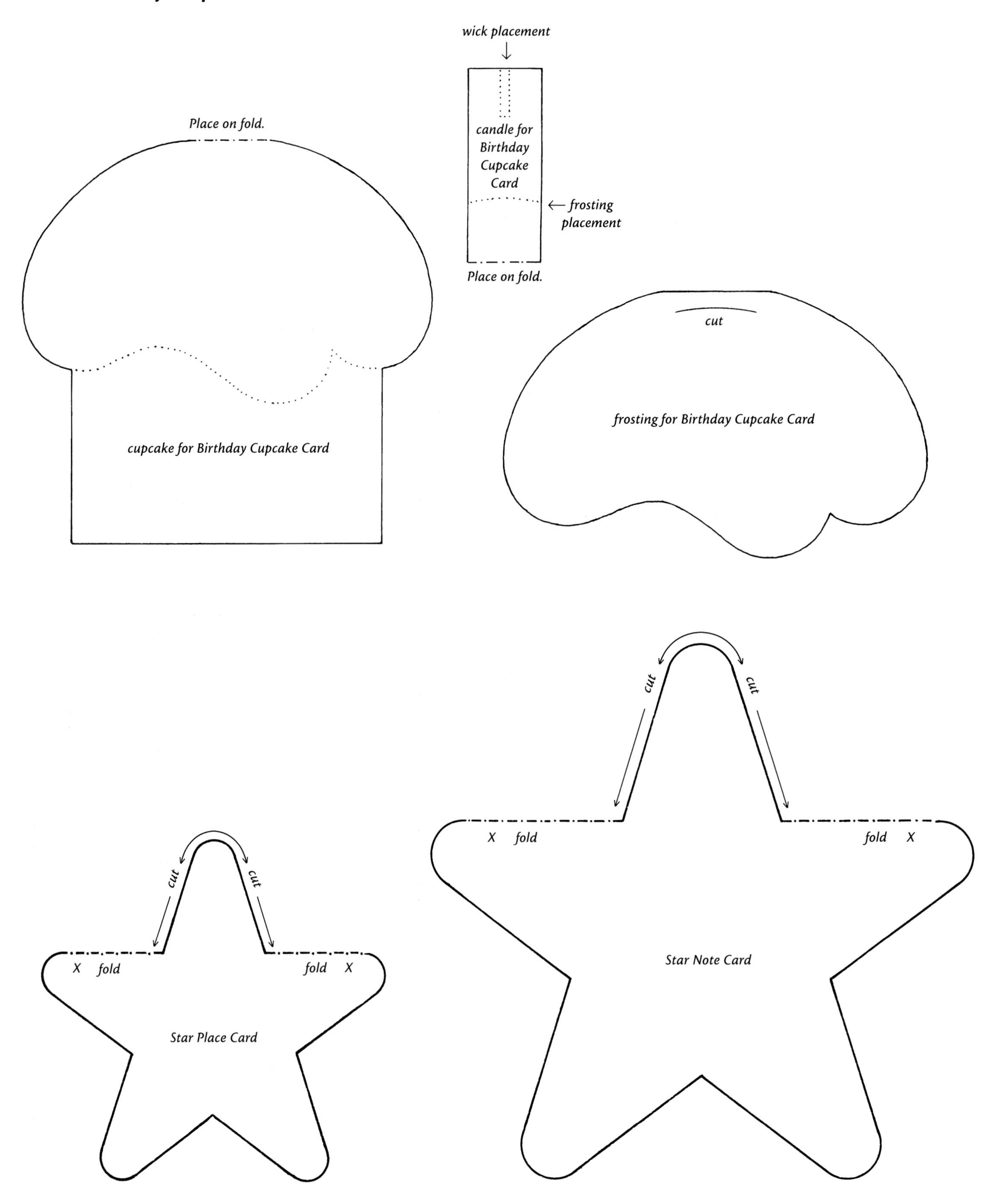

Etc Note and Pencil Note

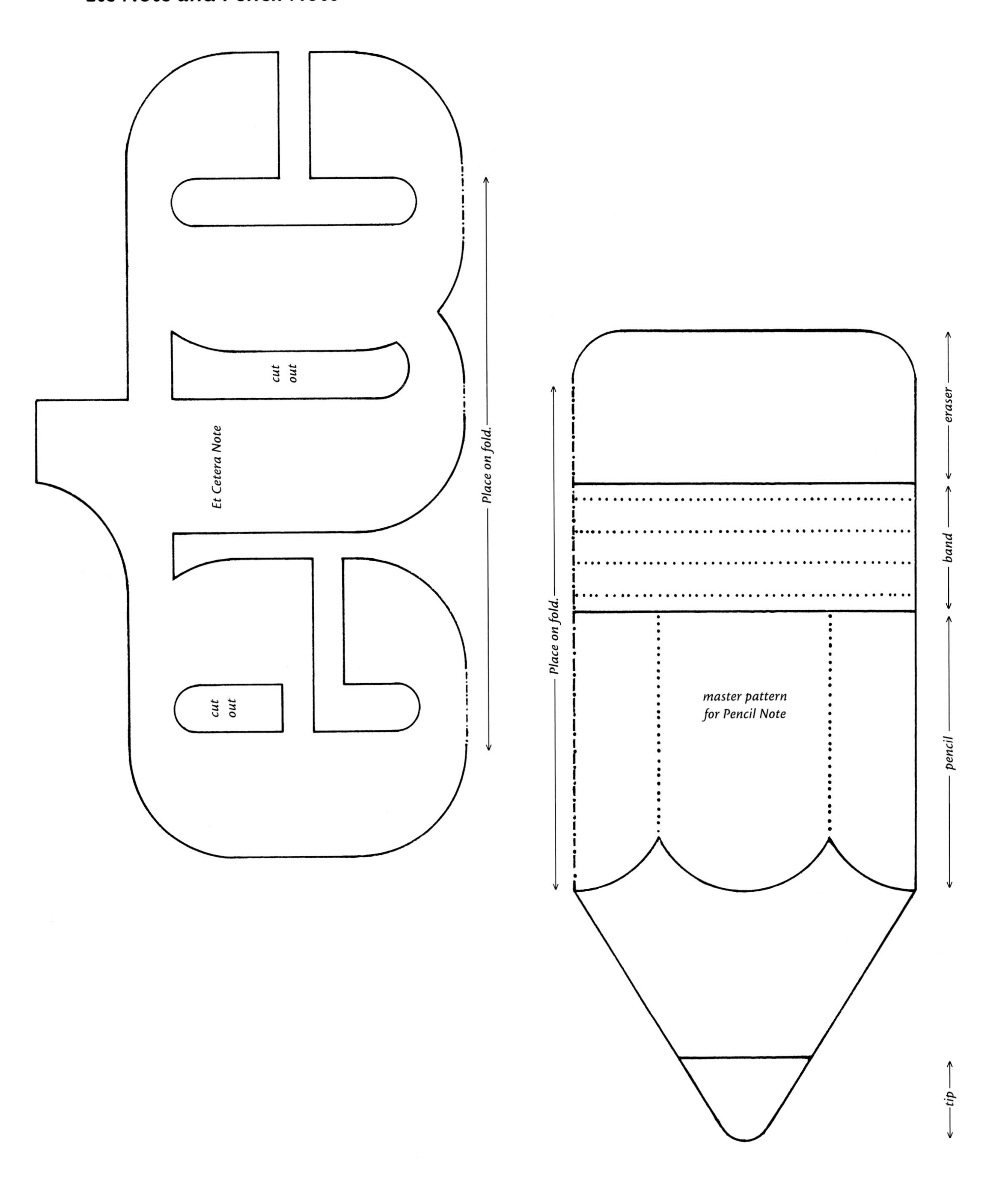

Candy Corn Invitation and Candy Corn Star

Align with bottom of white paper.

Candy Corn Invitation

Align with top of yellow paper.

Place on fold of pattern paper.

cut out

Align with folding line on Envelope D.

cat envelope liner for Candy Corn Invitation

← *folding line for card back*

star for Candy Corn Star

cut out

kernel for Candy Corn Star

Best Witches Card and Cat Card

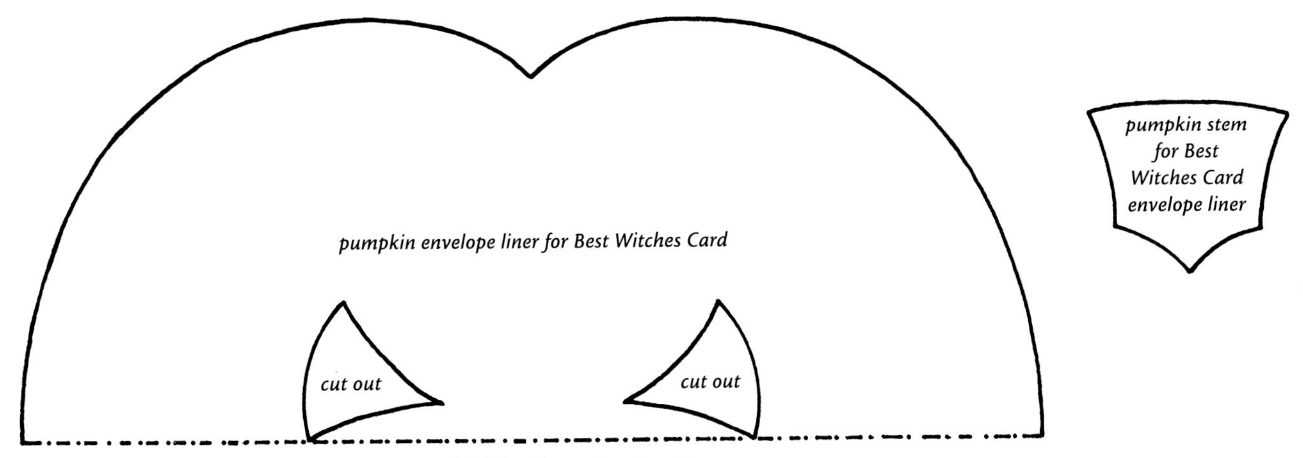

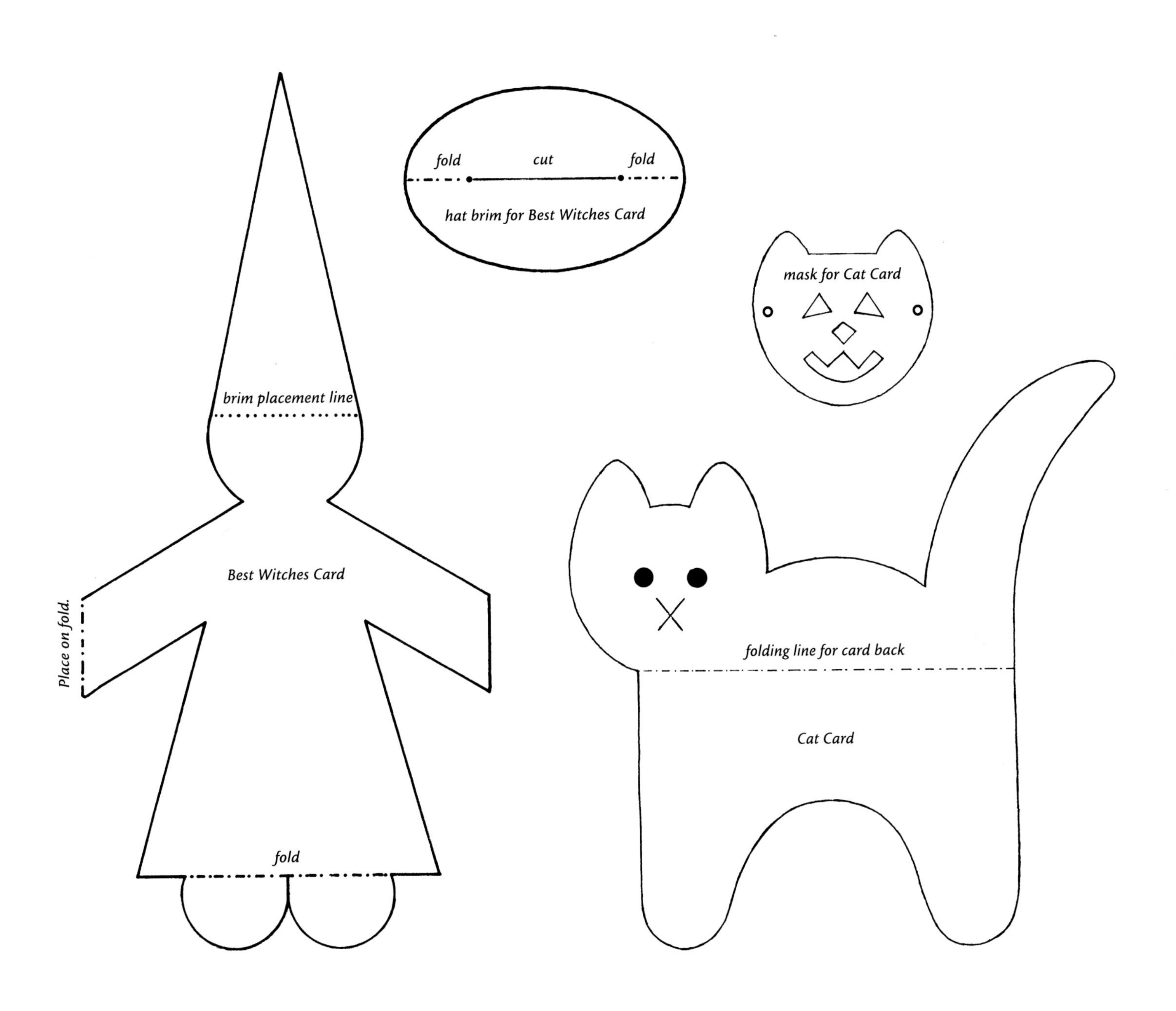

Apron Note Cards

Standing House Card

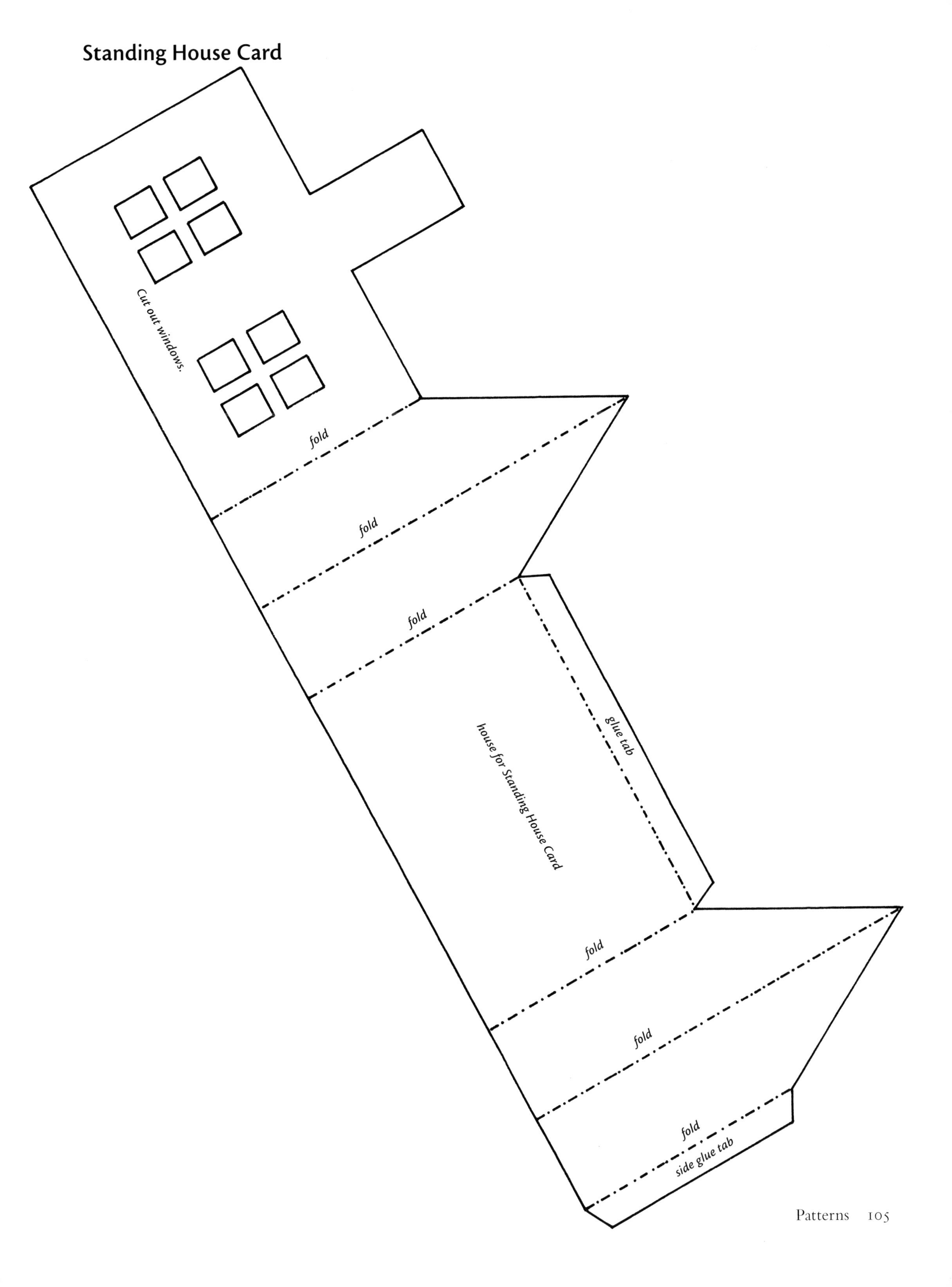

Standing House Card (continued) and Mashed Potatoes Card

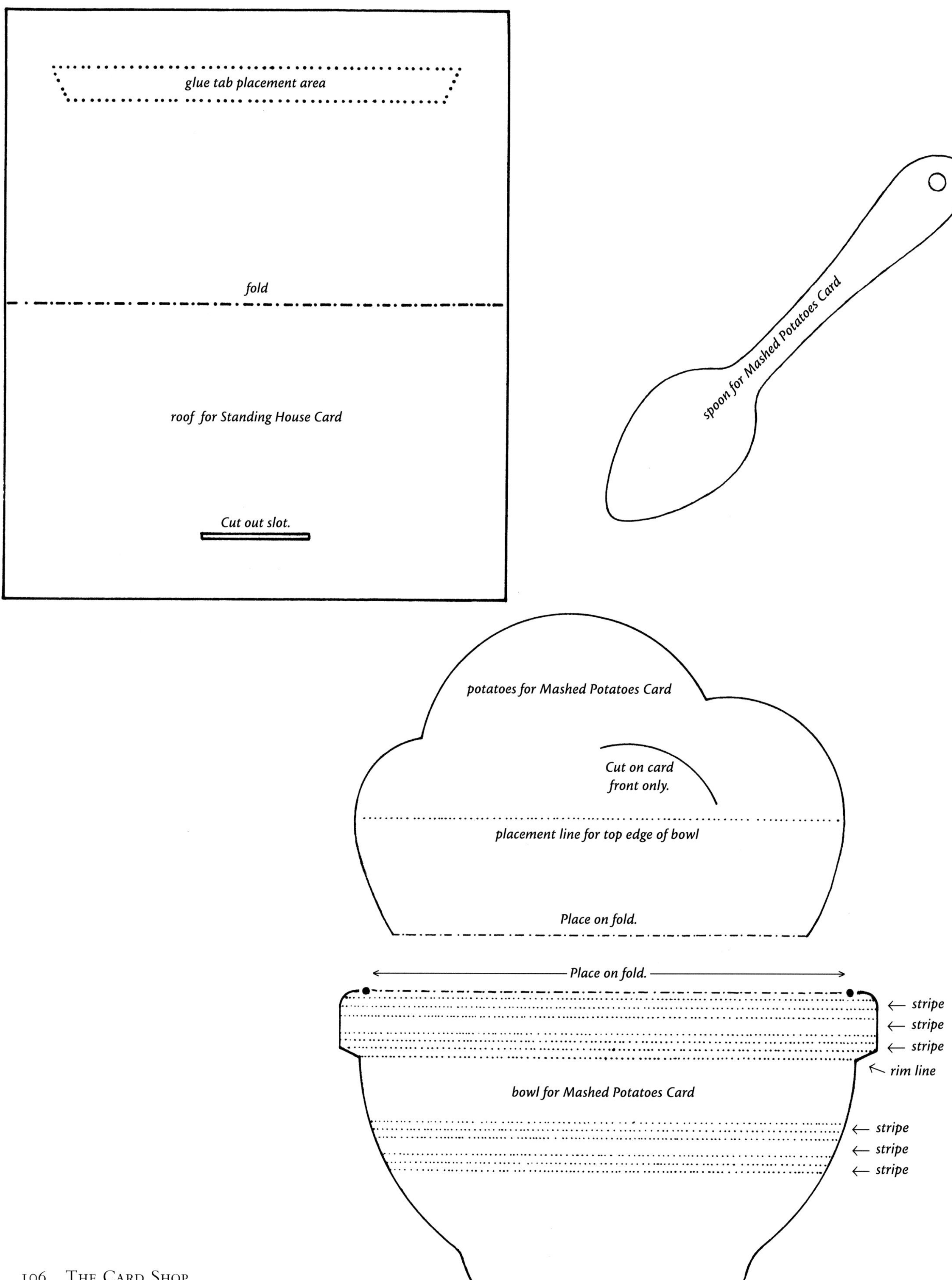

Crock Note and Get Well Teddy Card

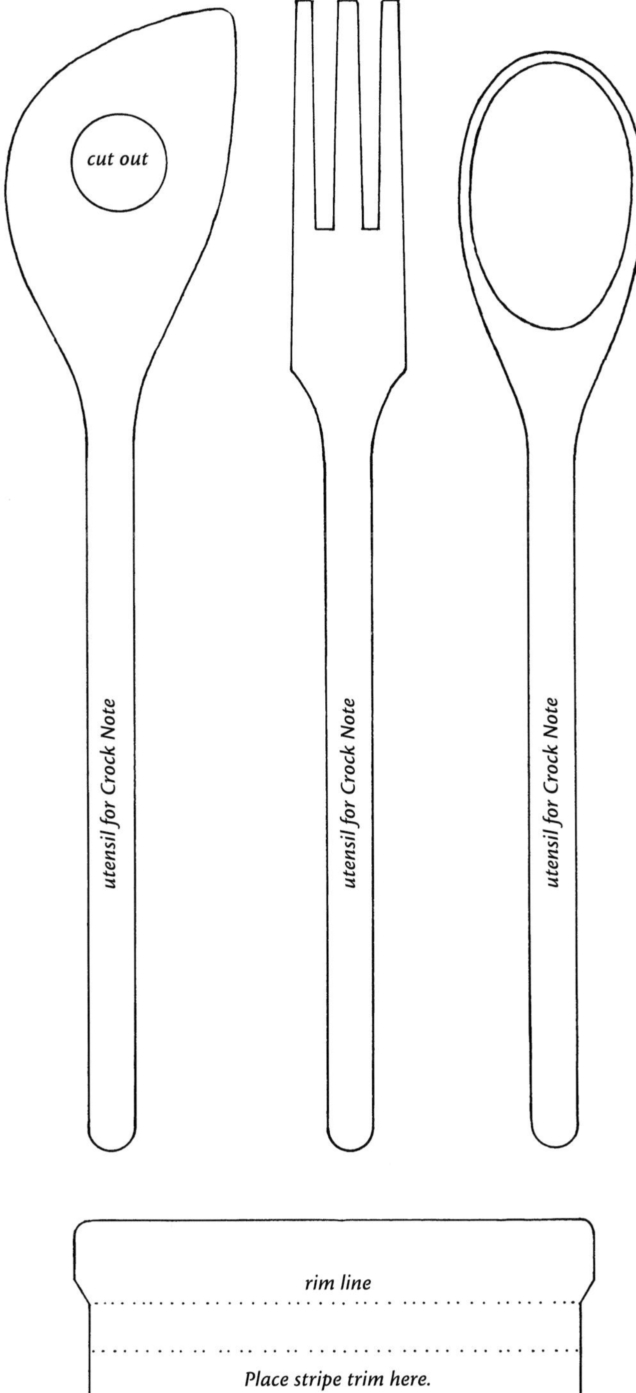

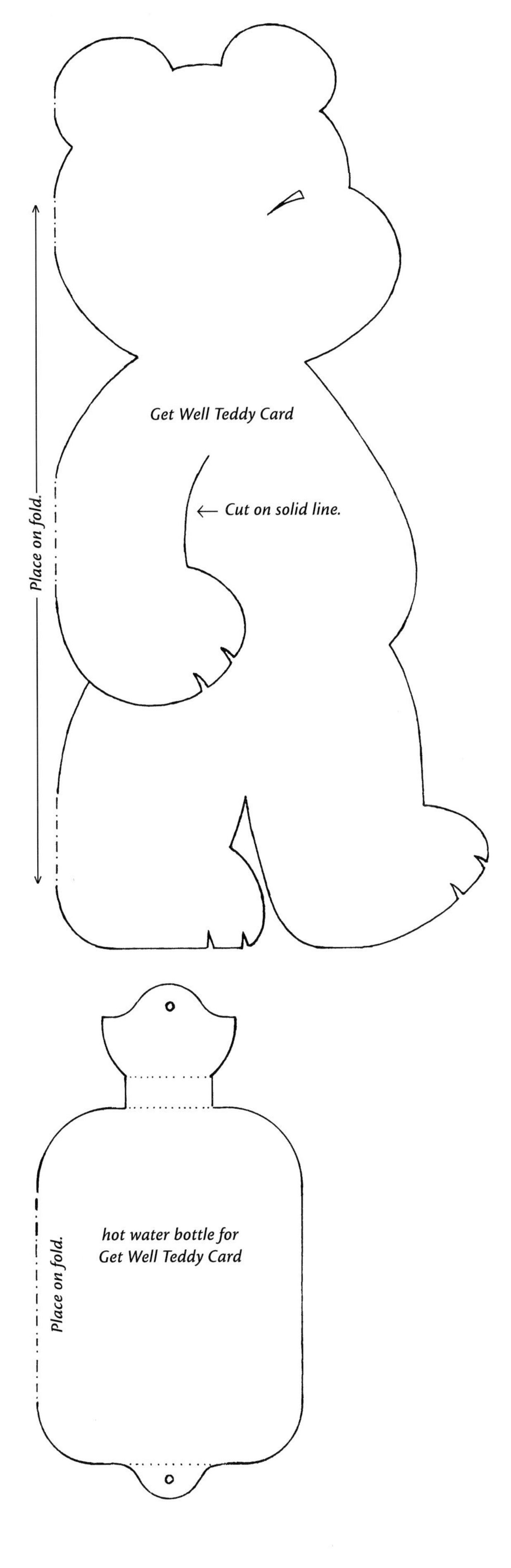

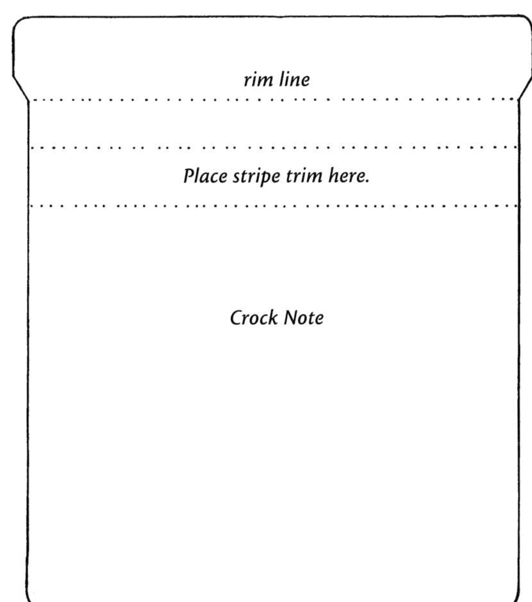

Snow Crystal Card

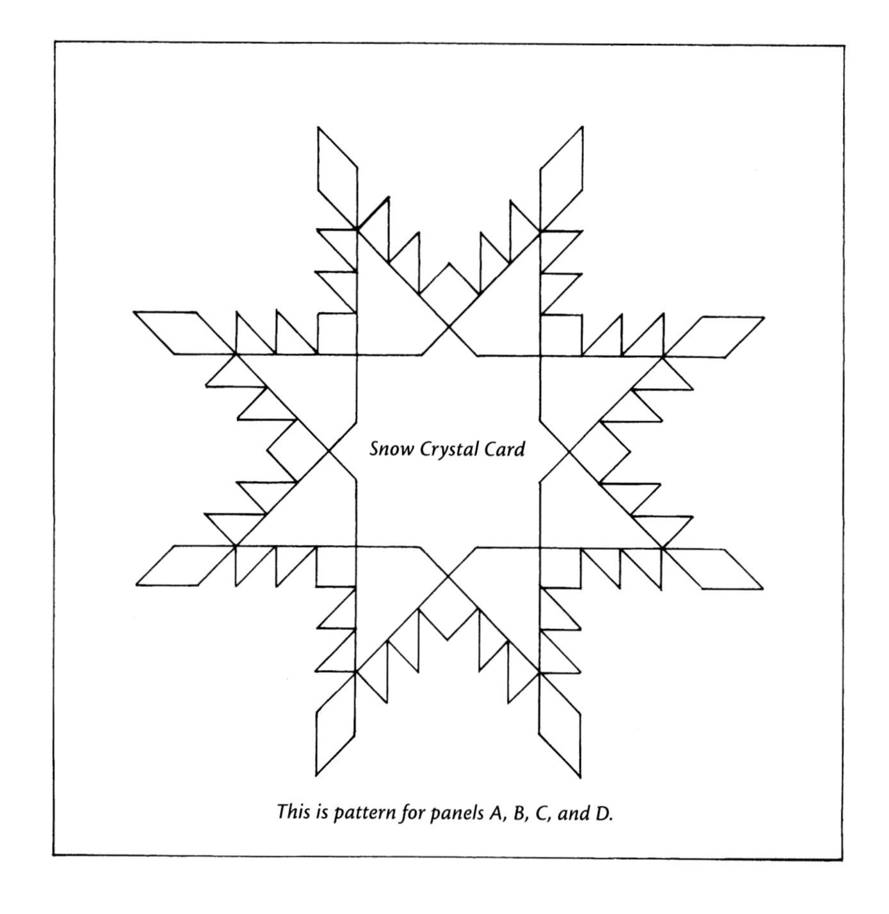

This is pattern for panels A, B, C, and D.

Sled card

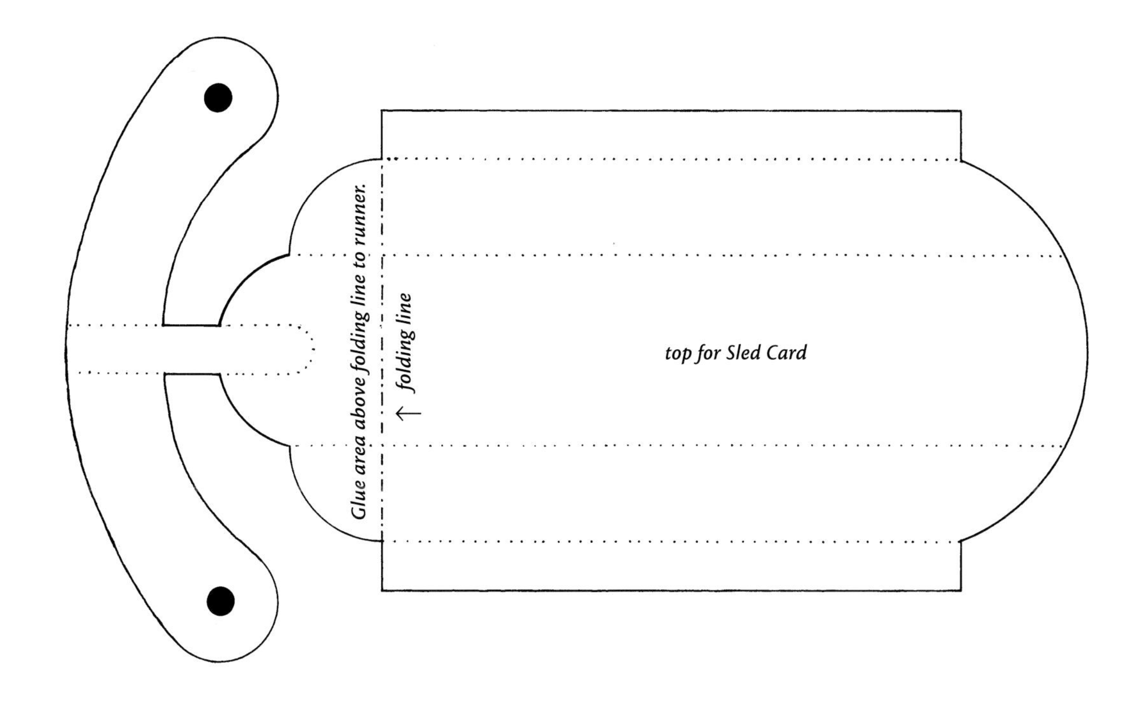
Glue area above folding line to runner.
↑ folding line
top for Sled Card

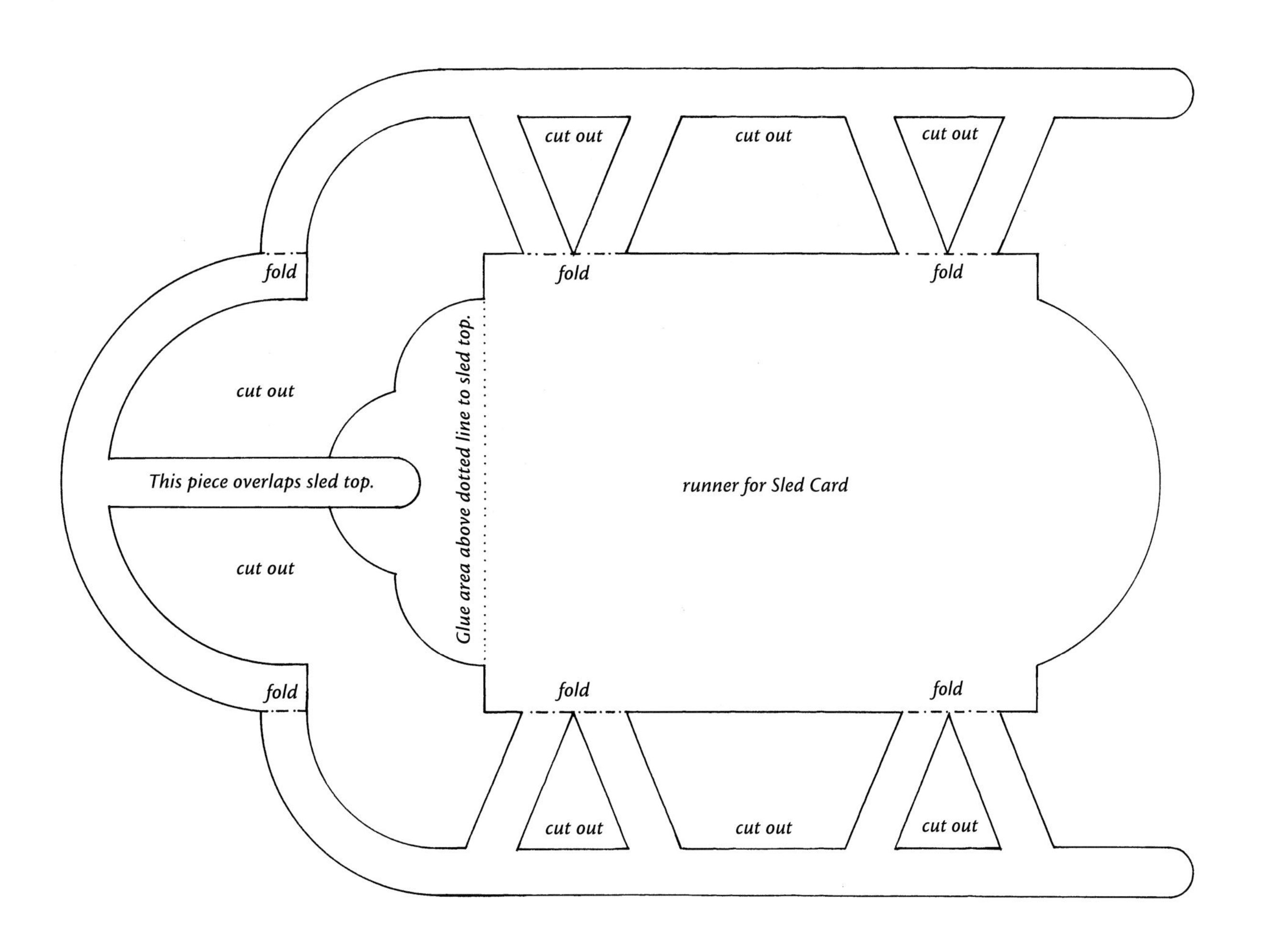
cut out
cut out
cut out
fold
fold
fold
cut out
Glue area above dotted line to sled top.
This piece overlaps sled top.
runner for Sled Card
cut out
fold
fold
fold
cut out
cut out
cut out

Woven House Card

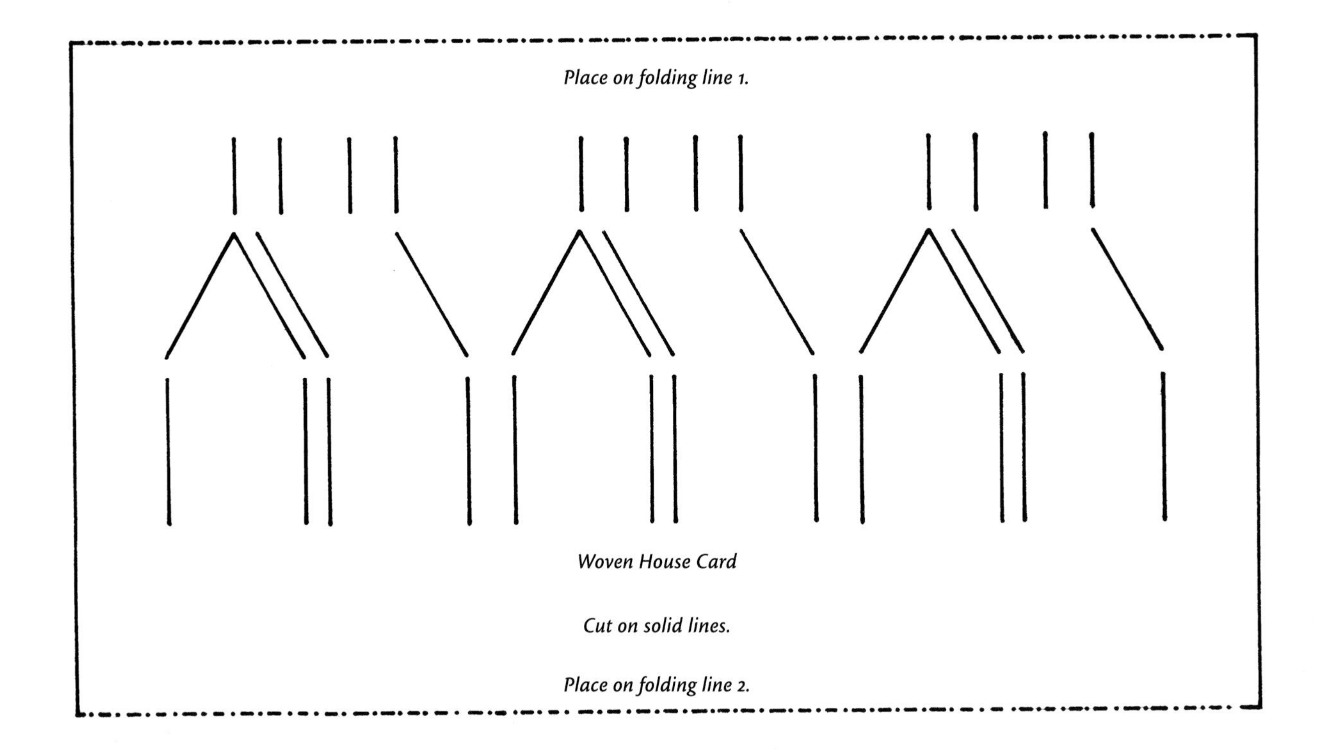

Christmas Cracker Card and Christmas Ball Card

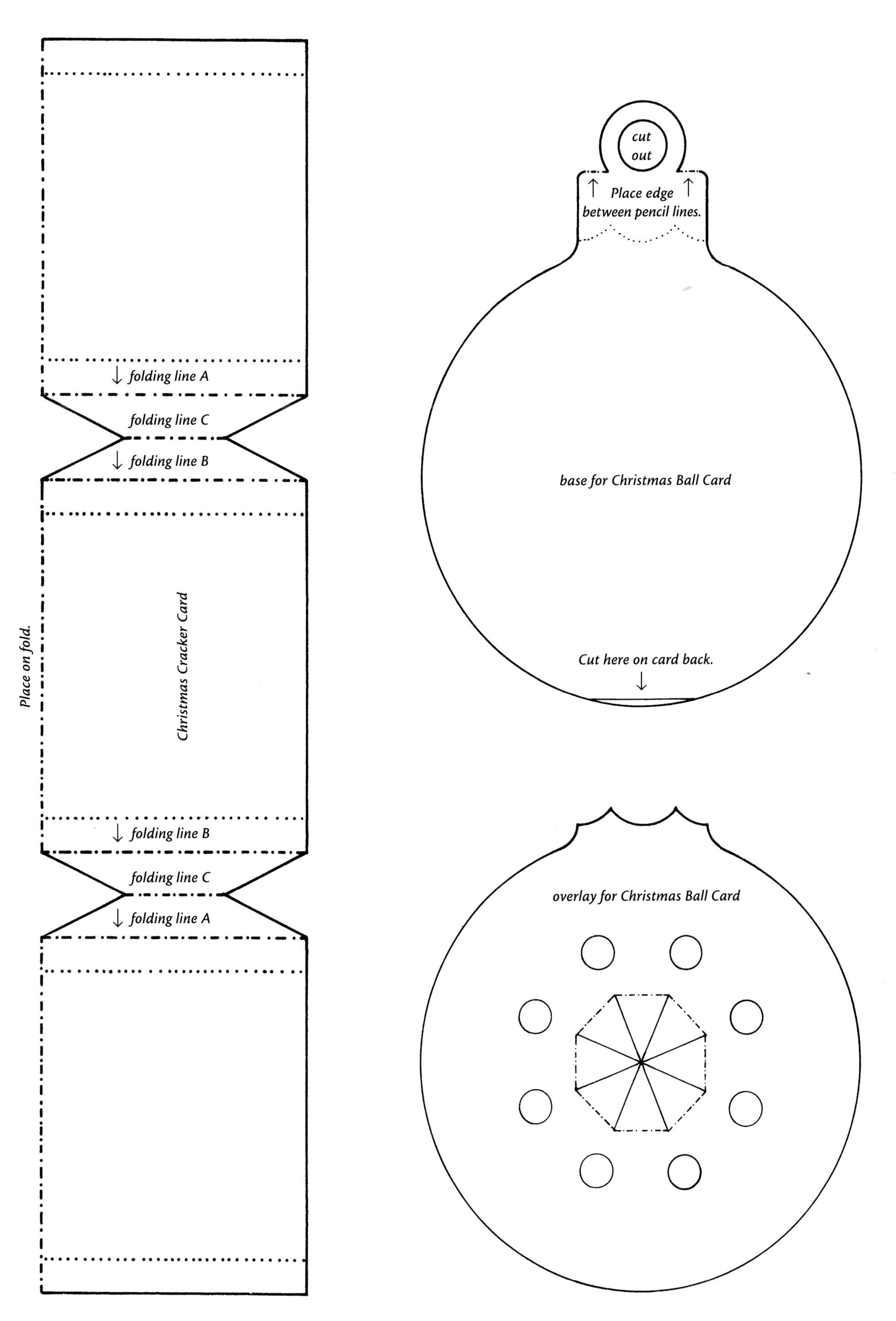

Hanukkah Menorah Card, Hanukkah Snowflake Card, and Santa Projects

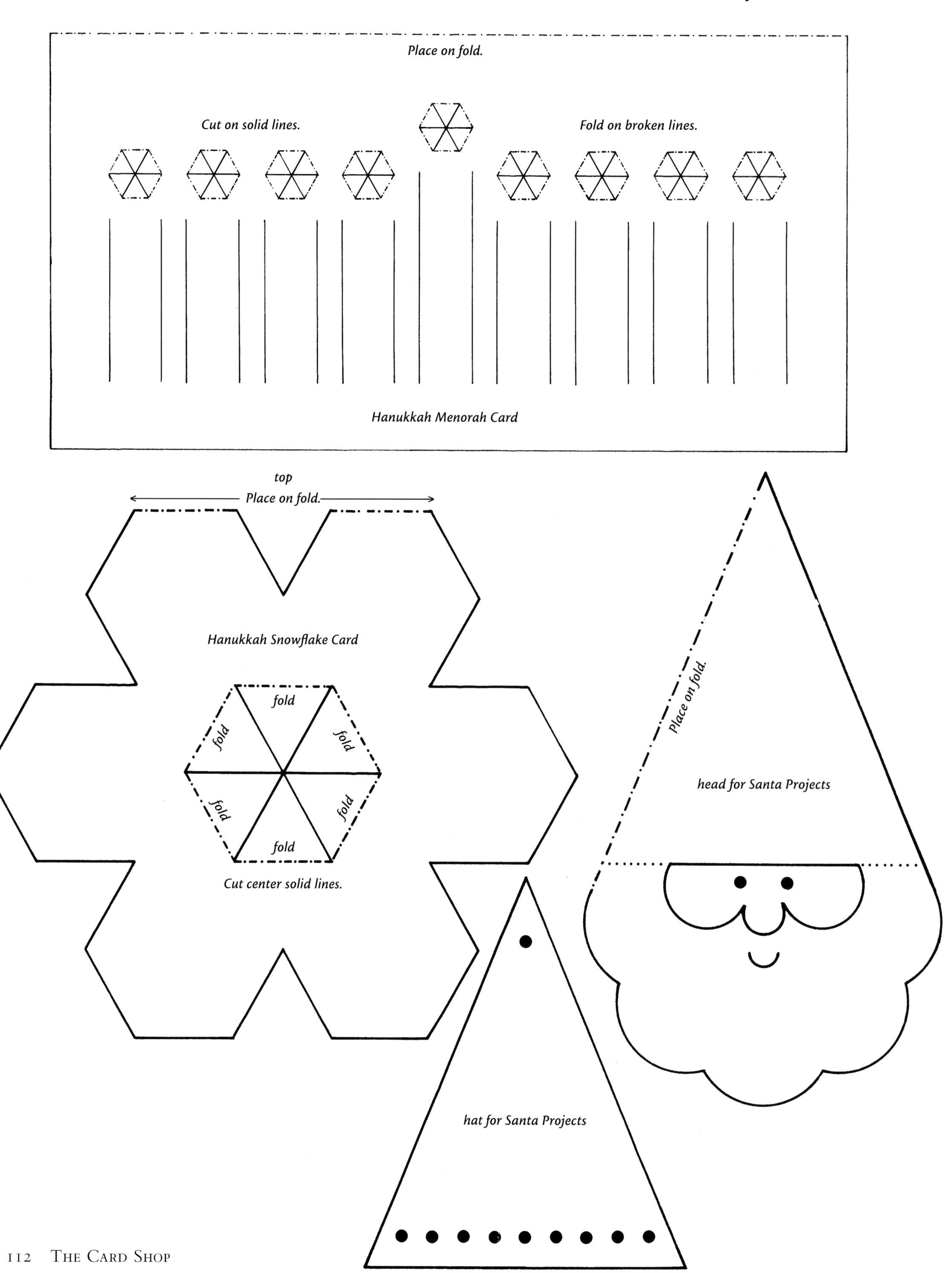

Ornament Cards

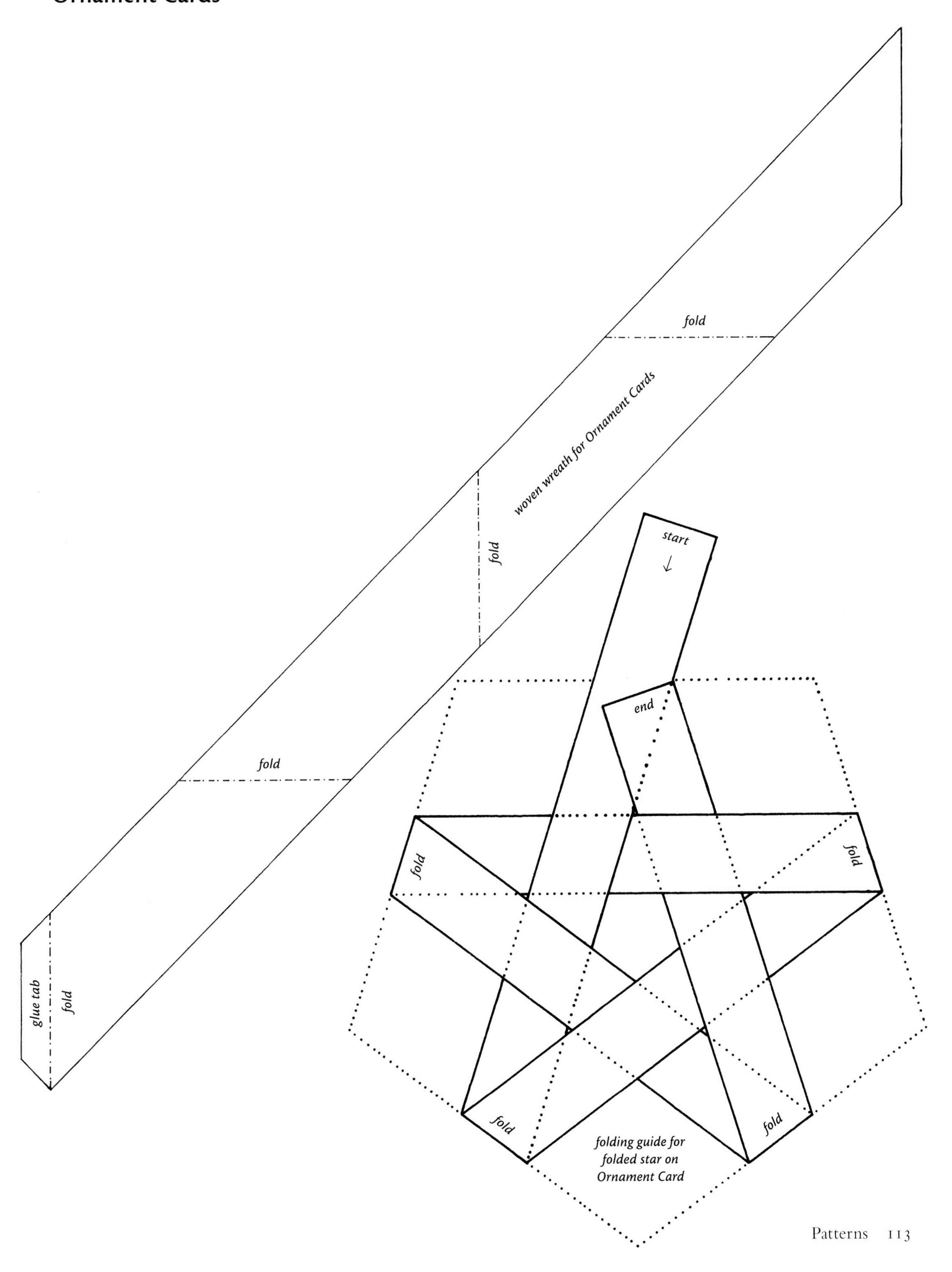

Garland of Snowmen Card

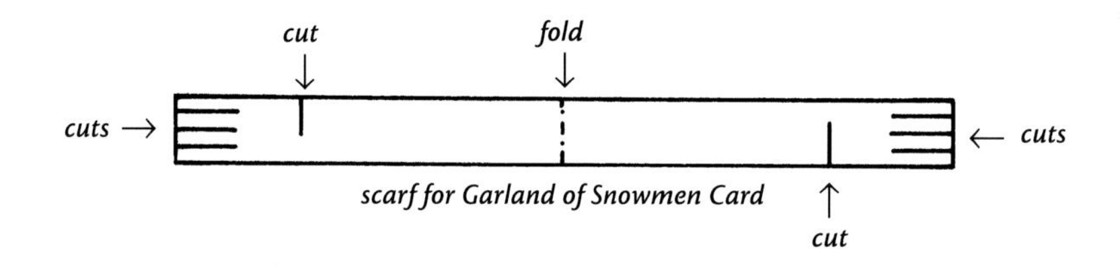

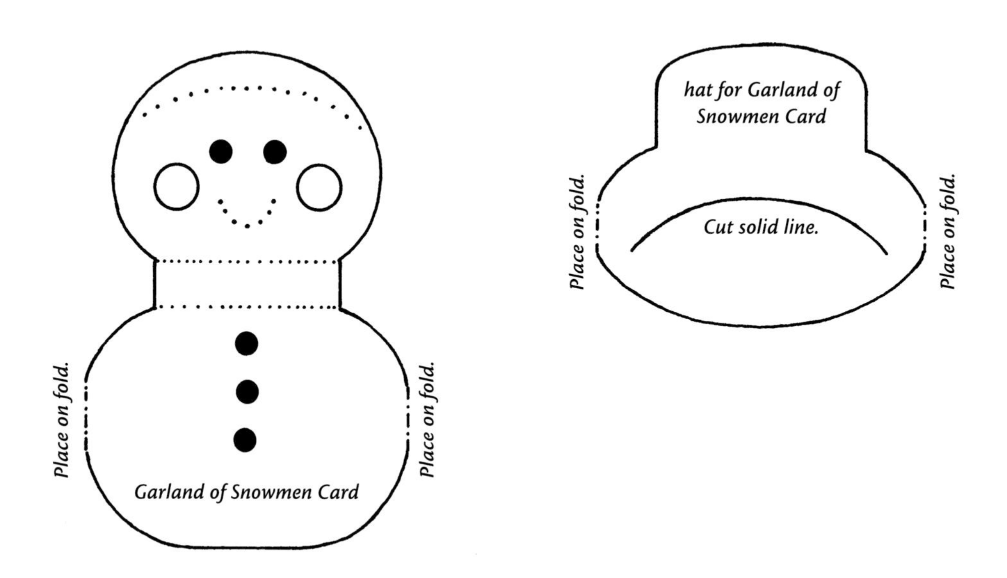